Rethinking Justice: Restoring Our Humanity

Richard H. Bell

Foreword by Walter Brueggemann

LEXINGTON BOOKS

A division of
ROWMAN & LITTLEFIELD PUBLISHERS, INC.
Lanham • Boulder • New York • Toronto • Plymouth, UK

LEXINGTON BOOKS

A division of Rowman & Littlefield Publishers, Inc.
A wholly owned subsidiary of The Rowman & Littlefield Publishing Group, Inc.
4501 Forbes Boulevard, Suite 200
Lanham, MD 20706

Estover Road
Plymouth PL6 7PY
United Kingdom

Copyright © 2007 by Lexington Books
First paperback edition 2008

British Library Cataloguing in Publication Information Available

Library of Congress Cataloging-in-Publication Data

Bell, Richard H., 1938–
  Rethinking justice : restoring our humanity / Richard H. Bell ; foreword by Walter
Brueggemann.
     p. cm.
  Includes bibliographical references and index.
  1. Justice. I. Title.
  JC578.B425 2007
  172'.2—dc22

                                                                2007011696

  ISBN-13: 978-0-7391-2228-0 (cloth : alk. paper)
  ISBN-10: 0-7391-2228-2 (cloth : alk. paper)
  ISBN-13: 978-0-7391-2229-7 (pbk. : alk. paper)
  ISBN-10: 0-7391-2229-0 (pbk. : alk. paper)

Printed in the United States of America

⊖™ The paper used in this publication meets the minimum requirements of American
National Standard for Information Sciences—Permanence of Paper for Printed Library
Materials, ANSI/NISO Z39.48–1992.

I dedicate this book to the Benedictine Sisters
of Holy Wisdom Monastery whose sense of justice as compassion
has served as an inspiration in the writing of this book,
and to Wilhelm Verwoerd who taught me to see the connections of
reconciliation and mercy to justice

How difficult it is to be just. We usually think of justice in terms of attribution and retribution, of allotting to everyone his due, but justice goes farther and claims more, much more from us. It begins at the moment when I see my neighbor (individual or collective) as different from me, at times irreducibly different, and recognizing his total right to be so, accept the fact that he is himself and has no reason to be merely a replica of myself.

Anthony Bloom,
Meditations: A Spiritual Journey Through the Parables

Justice appears in "that halt, that interval of hesitation, wherein lies all our consideration for our brothers in humanity."

Simone Weil, *The Iliad: Or the Poem of Force*

Contents

Contents

Foreword

The notion of justice has been around for a very long time. There is a firm, well-established notion of "justice as equity" that dominates thought, attention, and perception in the Western world. It grows out of Aristotle and specializes in "fairness," that each receives a "just reward." This tradition is greatly championed by those who style themselves as "critical realists." It also serves those who are the "enforcers" in society, the sort who in Northern Ireland are labeled "the strong men," and it feeds the "law and order" crowd that sees justice as a way to punish transgressors, keep people in their place, and maintain the status quo of present power arrangements. There is, of course, a great deal to be said on behalf of this tradition or it would not have flourished so well for so long. Clearly, every ignoble extrapolation from this tradition is not to be credited to the generators of such clear thinking public philosophy.

There is a great deal to be said for that notion of justice but, as Richard Bell makes clear in this splendid statement, not enough! Not enough, because "justice as equity" thinks formulaically about the public process and fails to take into serious account the specificity and pervasive concreteness of human suffering that sits under the radar of fairness, but that is the defining status of too many people and the inescapable outcome of too much public policy and public performance. Bell's characterization of such a tradition of justice, in the words of Stanley Cavell, is that we have "all fallen asleep," lulled into complacency amid advantage wherein systemic violence and concrete abuse are regarded as simply "normal" in social practice that gives people what they have coming to them. The insistence of Bell is that this philosophical tradition, with its immediately practical consequences, is not adequate. It needs not to be modified or extended, but rather contradicted by an alternative notion of justice that Bell finely lines out in these pages. If we have "all fallen asleep," then Bell is in the company of those who have, in parallel to Kant's phrasing, awakened from "dogmatic slumbers," for justice as fairness is indeed a "dogma" that commandeers facts to fit the scheme.

Bell's account of justice is a passionate, thoughtful, disciplined report on what happens to justice when we are "awakened." In Bell's articulation, the claims of "justice as fairness" are broadly and deeply challenged by "the facts on the ground" concerning suffering as a defining human reality, suffering that is in part generated by and in part legitimated by conventional structures of justice that do not notice or do not care or do not accept any responsibility for the outcomes of the public fabric in which we participate and from which we benefit. Thus Bell's important book lives at the interface of *the dominant philosophic tradition of justice* broadly assumed in the practice of social power and *the undeniable concrete human reality* of the twentieth century that is not reached or contained in the formal notion of "equity."

Bell's compelling summons is informed most especially by Simone Weil with her advocacy of resistance to "the empire of force" and by Martha Nussbaum with her mandate for moral imagination that may impinge upon the public practice of justice. The large horizon of Bell's data, about which we do not often enough want to think, is the deep unnamed and mostly unacknowledged human suffering that is the undeniable outcome of colonial exploitation, racist policies, and sexist practices. Any one of the contexts of such suffering is more than one can stomach when one draws close to savaged human bodies. But take them all together, the sum of violence in the name of fairness is nearly beyond imagination, even though Bell, following Weil, invites us to such imagination.

Given the undeniable world of imposed human pain, Bell's concrete case study comes from his extended periods of study in South Africa and his specific engagement with the Truth and Reconciliation Commission that, in a not fully rational and systematic way, permitted human suffering to be voiced, allowed deep violence to be exhibited and confessed, and made room for forgiveness in the public process. Out of that uncommon experience came the public awareness that mercy, compassion, and forgiveness are not maudlin, romantic ideas, but they are the indispensable public stuff out of which human community can survive, prosper, and move beyond its seasons of destructiveness. The reason such practice is indispensable in the public process is that it belongs to human persons in human community to be connected to each other in thick ways that are not covered by retribution, equity, or revenge, even if the revenge is occasioned by the state. It is this full recognition of humanness that has been excessively thinned in the rational tradition of equity that must now be given attention and credence. Bell cites some rhetoric around "the Cuban missile crisis" to make clear that beyond superpower posturing and ideological confrontation, there were fragile, courageous human agents at work who were able to avoid the drive to mutual destructiveness. While Reinhold Niebuhr's classic assignment of "love" and "justice" to "proper spheres" of individual and society continues to be instructive, Bell's argument, based on the realities of human suffering and human hope in concrete cases, suggests that matters are not so readily sorted out as that Niebuhrian tradition would suggest.

In the end Bell insists, within a broad human tradition, that the "right" to justice must be grounded in the "obligation" to justice, "a shared obligation to the well-being of one's fellow human beings". For all the clear thinking critical ethical and juridical thinkers, it is not unimportant that the likes of Desmond Tutu and Vaclav Havel finally are our most compelling teachers about human possibility. They knew the philosophic tradition, but are primally informed by the truth of human bodies in the face of anti-human power that may be "legitimate" but that lacks the credibility of truthfulness. Bell might have cited many other cases, notably the Israeli-Palestinian crisis, the Northern Ireland troubles, the index of incest in the United States, the continuing racist, class divide in the U.S. economy, and so on. But the case is clear. Justice must be rethought from the bottom of violated bodies up to more compassionate policy formation. Bell's is a major contribution in this direction, a wake-up call to restoration of our humanity that has respect for human suffering.

Walter Brueggemann
Columbia Theological Seminary
December 19, 2006

Preface

Following the lead of Socrates and Wittgenstein, I believe that philosophy is essentially a form of conversation. Philosophy as a conversation searches for the clarification of concepts and engages in a mutual quest for understanding— an understanding of our common humanity within the contexts of our cultural difference. In the conversations that have gone on for centuries about the concept of justice, philosophers have ranged widely in their understanding of this concept. In this book I sort through a number of the conversations that have taken place historically and contemporaneously on justice and lift up what I believe to be some of the best moments in those conversations.

Besides having read and taught "standard views" on the concept of justice in Plato, Aristotle, Kant, Rousseau, Mill, Nietzsche, and Rawls, I entered more actively into *the conversation about justice* upon reading the writings of the twentieth-century French philosopher Simone Weil in the 1970s and, subsequently, the writings of Vaclav Havel following the fall of communism and the transformation of eastern Europe to democracy after 1989. A third pivotal moment was reading about and following closely the establishment of and the ongoing process for national reconciliation laid out in the South African Truth and Reconciliation Commission (TRC) beginning in 1994. Here were three examples—conversations regarding justice—that challenged the normal discussions too often found in Western philosophical literature. I subsequently spent most of a year engaged in research in South Africa in 2000. During that year I participated in a graduate seminar on "Justice" led by Wilhelm Verwoerd at the University of Stellenbosch. Wilhelm had recently returned to his philosophy teaching post after two years as a researcher for the TRC and helping to draft its final report. The conversations on justice I had with him that surrounded the TRC were dramatic, fresh, and challenging to any I had previously experienced. What was surprising, however, was that these conversations frequently echoed the urgings of Simone Weil—urgings with which I was very familiar—to move toward "a new virtue of justice." These experiences have since focused my teaching and research around *rethinking justice* and have led to the writing of this book. I discovered as I engaged in this new philosophical conversation that earlier research and writing I had done on Wittgenstein, Simone Weil, Vaclav Havel, Alasdair MacIntyre, and others had laid a foundation to differently envision this conversation.

Our world, too, has changed dramatically since 1989 and requires new global and cross-cultural strategies in our thinking about justice. Many philosophers, contemporary writers, and political leaders, as well as human rights organizations and community-based non-governmental organizations (NGOs), have reshaped the conversation on justice in the past decade or more and this book takes into account some of the more salient voices in that recent conversation.

I am indebted to many students and colleagues at the University of Cambridge where I first began writing this book, and to students and colleagues in the United States and southern Africa for challenging many of my assumptions and forcing greater clarity in my own rethinking of justice. I am particularly grateful for the opportunity to teach at Rhodes University in Grahamstown, South Africa, during a term from September through mid-November, 2004, and again for a semester from mid-July to mid-December, 2006, under a Fulbright lecture-research grant. There I encountered honors and masters students eager to discuss justice issues linked directly to what they called "the transformation to a new South Africa" and the personal stake they had in such discussions. This experience affirmed the value of the issues taken up in this book for future generations, and sharpened a number of arguments linked especially to its latter chapters.

Finally, I also wish to thank Anne Jacqueline Guthrie, a graduate of the College of Wooster who has provided critical assistance in the preparation of this book—especially for her work in helping to prepare the Selected Bibliography and the Index, and Rianna Oelofsen, a Ph.D. candidate at Rhodes, whose critical questions and discussions often focused some of my ideas. My wife, Barbara Bell has exercised her excellent critical eye on the form and style of late versions of this text and made it a more readable book. She has also been a patient companion through a rough period of surgical recovery I experienced in the midst of writing this book.

Richard H. Bell
Cambridge and Grahamstown, 2004
Wooster and Grahamstown, 2005 and 2006

Introduction

Philosophy's virtue is responsiveness. What makes it philosophy is not
that its response will be total, but that it will be tireless, awake when others have all fallen asleep.

[Stanley Cavell, *This New Yet Unapproachable America:*
Lectures after Emerson after Wittgenstein]

When it comes to thinking about and understanding "justice" we in the Western post-Enlightenment world "have fallen asleep." We have lost the virtue of
responsiveness. There seems to be a loss, or at least a failure of vision, regarding what it means to be *a just human being*—to practice a sense of justice in our ordinary lives with others. The reflections found in this book are a
series of attentive exercises in responsiveness to the concept of justice. Henry
David Thoreau wrote in *Walden*: "You only need sit still long enough in some
attractive spot in the woods that all its inhabitants may exhibit themselves to
you by turns." And Stanley Cavell says of Thoreau's remark: "All of *Walden*
is condensed in these few drops."[1] *Walden* is asking us to exercise the power
of stillness, of silence, of being present to what surrounds us—in one instance
nature, in another human beings, and another our human communities. This
exercise also reminds us of the importance of our being present to our use of
concepts like "justice" and "injustice," "tyranny," and "democracy," "harmdoing," and "compassion." Thoreau wants us, in Cavell's words, to "take up
residence" before whatever may present itself to us. What is present to us here
is the concept of justice and how we have neglected or fallen asleep before it.

The very idea of justice should be a testament to our humanity. Rather, the
idea of justice seems to follow political, ideological, or religious dogma
throughout the world. Instead of promoting or restoring a sense of human

1

well-being and peace, community reconciliation, and an individual sense of virtuous living, justice has come to reflect a more retributive spirit and too often reflects an abuse of power. This book surveys the many sides of justice and steers the reader, on the one hand, to a more traditional, or classical, sense of justice that suggests true justice would encourage that less harm and greater good be done toward our fellow human beings; that justice should reflect what is good in our very nature. On the other hand, this book points to a number of new horizons for our rethinking justice—horizons shaped by courageous political and moral revolutions in our own time.

Each chapter is designed to awaken the reader to some different aspect of the meaning of justice that has fallen away from it in our time and our culture, and to expose the reader to numerous narrative perspectives on justice found in classical and contemporary literature and as expressed in the stories and ordinary lives of human beings and their communities around the world. This exposé will open out the philosophical virtue of responsiveness. Our humanity is bound to our moral responsiveness and is indebted to something other than ourselves. All the voices you will encounter in these pages believe that human life as a moral and spiritual enterprise is essentially *responsive*.[2] The concept of justice gives expression to its meaning as we are responsive to its demands.

We are all given good reason and many occasions to think about justice. It seems clear that we can identify many instances of *injustice*: immense disparity in wealth and poverty, wanton violence with little accountability, heightened cycles of revenge with no clear end in sight, abuse of power between races, ethnic groups, men and women, and a growing distrust between global neighbors and religious traditions. With so much injustice at hand it seems reasonable to ask: Where is the *justice* to respond to such *injustice*? Do we, however, have a clear conception of what justice is? Searching for a response to these questions I turned to a number of recent books and articles dealing with both the philosophical and legal aspects of "justice." Among these was a book titled *What Is Justice? Classic and Contemporary Readings*.[3] It is one of a very few texts with primary readings from the world's greatest philosophers and religious thinkers covering well over three millennia. Its overwhelming focus, however, is on justice in Western political and philosophical thought from the eighteenth-century Enlightenment to the present, though it does give a token nod to *The Koran* and Chinese texts.

A recurring theme in this reader is that the idea of justice can be understood as a variation on the expressions "giving one their due" or "balancing the scales" and finding appropriate or proportional retribution for "righting" a wrong done. This is characteristically what one can also find in the *Old Testament*, *The Koran*, and in much of ancient Greek literature as well as in the modern Western (post-Enlightenment) theories of justice. There is, however, considerable literature to show that some of the earlier ideas of justice, especially the Greek idea of justice, were more richly textured than suggested in the brief selections in this text. For example, in fifth-century BC Athenian society and earlier, punishment was often highly deliberated and tempered by compassion and pity. Suffering, too, might give rise to hesitation in judgment and punishment, and as we will discuss later, the Greeks, not satisfied with justice being an individual concern, gave birth to the idea of "civil society" in the West. Subsequent Roman philosophers discussed the place of "mercy" or "clemency" in legal justice. Clearly there are also strong strains of mercy, compassion, and forgiveness in the biblical conceptions of justice. We shall examine these more richly textured accounts more closely.

The theme of retribution for a wrong done is strongly carried into eighteenth-century Enlightenment views of justice and "modern Western" jurisprudence. Whether justice is conceived in such narrow retributive terms or more broadly, it seems clear to say that historically the idea of justice has been thought to be a leading virtue in societies—if not *the* primary virtue. Michael Sandel notes: "Justice is primary in that the demands of justice outweigh other moral and political interests . . . [it] is the highest of social virtues, the one that must be met before other [values] can make their claims."[4] Then why is it so difficult to think about what justice is? Australian philosopher Raimond Gaita says, "Justice is a value which straddles the moral and the political realms."[5] That is to say that justice should figure into how our actions to other persons are measured and judged to be good, and also how we structure what is a reasonable and humane way to manage our communal affairs. There is, however, less clarity and agreement as to what the concept "moral action" means here and what "goods" it serves in societies.

What, for example, do we learn about justice morally and politically in the following case? You may have read in the September 26, 2003, *New York Times* front page story that Amina Lawal in Nigeria finally "got her due." You remember she had been sentenced to death by stoning under Islamic law for committing adultery. After awaiting her execution for two years she has now been acquitted by a higher Islamic court. Many say this is a victory for justice, but the grounds for the acquittal seem to have little to do with justice and from the beginning there seemed to be no equity between Ms. Lawal and the man who fathered her child—not to mention the issue of proportionality of punishment to "the crime." In the end her sentence was overturned on technicalities—and a whole lot of bad worldwide publicity. Curiously it seemed not to occur to the judges in either the first judgment or the second, for example, to have pity or to consider "mercy" as a part of legal justice (though mercy has a small place in classical Islamic law), or whether "justice" in this case is serving a moral good. Justice does not seem to be thought of as a part of the moral or social fabric of a society, as a social virtue.

Most conceptions of law and justice worldwide would condemn her first sentence as "unjust"—it seemed wildly disproportionate to the crime. Interestingly, if you read the scores of essays on foundations of justice in Western literature you also discover that the idea of "getting one's due" as this was encoded into rules of law only applied *to some* in society—primarily to its male members. This is true in the literature of Aristotle, Hobbes, Hume, Kant, and Hegel (to name a few). Also, going back to Hume and Hegel, and especially Kant, these thinkers took pains to make it explicit that the rule of law and all "rational" ideas of fairness under the law applied only to white, Western males. One wonders what happened to the idea of equality and human dignity *for all* in their discussions?[6]

Remember, this is all part of the literature that backs up many of our contemporary ideas of "justice." Ironically it also formed the background to justify colonialism for some 500 years—from early human slave trade to recent apartheid regimes. We shall be examining the residual effects of colonialism with regard to how "others" or distant strangers are treated today—especially across cultures, how we understand the concept of equality of former colonized peoples, and how the present state of our global social and moral economy understands the idea of justice. Insofar as we claim that justice is the intellectual backbone of what we call "modern enlightened" civilizations, we are left to ask with respect to both local and global justice: *What is due and to whom?*

More troubling than what the historical texts provide us for thinking about justice is how the contemporary philosophical discussion seems to be stuck on either criticizing, defending, or amending post-Kantian views like those of John Rawls or of various utilitarian or libertarian views.[7] These recent discussions focus around views that apply primarily to empirical or rational grounds to support individual "rights" in Western democracies, and dispute natural "endowments" and individual "entitlements" with some attention given to the relationship of the individual to community (distributive economic and social justice issues). In all these discussions the nature of the debates are what John Dunn calls "practically inert."

Dunn, in his thought-provoking book *Western Political Theory in the Face of the Future*, writes:

Today the intellectual custodians of our moral, spiritual or aesthetic aspirations scarcely trouble themselves with the question of what it is reasonable to expect [in thinking about justice]. Modern philosophical theories of justice, accordingly, are not for the most part actively misleading. Instead, they are simply idle: practically inert.[8]

He suggests that we need a fresh outlook on justice that "contains the resources to show us how the future can be made less grim."[9] I will argue that part of the solution to our thinking about justice is reminding ourselves how "grim" the recent past has been and the future can be because of our present moral and political preoccupations. We must also recover the right moral and spiritual resources—a new qualitative responsiveness—to show how the future can be made more just. Only then will we be in a position to steer in a more hopeful (and less grim) direction.

Our approach to "rethinking justice" is to surface what John Dunn called the human "moral, spiritual and aesthetic aspirations" in order to texture the debate more highly; to force our rethinking around concepts like trust, obligation, suffering and injustice, mercy, poverty, human dignity and equality, compassion and reconciliation. It is not that these concepts have not entered into some current discussions of justice, but they have been marginalized and are often deemed too romantic or "soft," or thought to idealize the discussions. The list, however, of those who have focused on such concepts with respect to justice are not themselves "soft" thinkers, nor romantics or political idealists; they do, however, see the importance of "moral, spiritual, and aesthetic aspirations" of human beings everywhere. Theorists and practitioners of such justice include: Simone Weil, Peter Winch, Jonathan Glover, Martha Nussbaum, Amartya Sen, Luce Irigaray, Alasdair MacIntyre, Onora O'Neill, Immanuel Levinas, Stanley Cavell, Vaclav Havel, Nelson Mandela, and others.

Throughout this book the reader will frequently encounter the vision of the French political philosopher Simone Weil [1909–1943] on justice as she charted an unusually challenging—if not radical—course for rethinking what she called "a new virtue of justice." She wrote during the period between the two World Wars in the twentieth century—a period when the shadows of fascism and communism were spreading across the globe. Although her views on justice are not known as widely as they should be, they are far from "idle" or "inert." Her manner of formulating the issues and presenting challenges will help shape our rethinking of justice.[10]

The above list of philosophers, among others, often appear to be working against the main stream of modern ethical and political thought of the past few decades; working to illuminate the confusion that has lead our humanity to the edge of an abyss. Stanley Cavell speaks for such philosophers when he recovers and reformulates Emerson's "perfectionism" and identifies a "search for directions in what seems a scene of moral chaos, the scene of the dark place in which one has lost one's way."[11]

Finding one's way in thinking about justice is the central thesis of this book. "Finding" implies a sense of having been lost, and finding one's way requires direction—direction given by philosophers, civic leaders, an array of ordinary human beings, and by listening carefully to one's own humanity. As such directions are woven into this book they refocus our human sensibilities to one another, allowing a reflective recovery of one's way of being human. The reader will encounter conversation and demonstration—a kind of saying and showing as Wittgenstein might say—examples as a testament to our humanity. The very democratic enterprise that surrounds the meaning of justice is a process of self-reflection that brings into view our selves *with* our neighbors, friends, and distant strangers.

The history itself of the past century, of course, has shaped many of our current conceptions of what it means to be just. We shall also move to some new territories for thinking about justice. For example, we will explore challenges provided us by the growing presence of "restorative justice" initiatives in several countries and as it was developed in the South African Truth and Reconciliation Commission. Also, in the light of the post 1989 "victory" of more democratic polity over communism—especially in eastern Europe— there is concern with how best the economic resources of our new "global culture" can be equitably distributed and how new forms of imperialism and totalitarianism can be avoided. Thus the discussions of justice in political and economic development strategies, and justice across borders or comparative views of justice, are gaining in interest. The following chapters will draw insight from the thinkers mentioned above—and others—and from recent history and literature to understand what it means "to be just" and to enrich and challenge our thinking about the concept of justice.

In the end I want to ask what are the spiritual parameters that surround our talk about justice? Where does the language of some forms of religious belief and spirituality intersect with the debates about rethinking justice and an understanding of a more deliberative democracy? I will argue that the very concept of spirituality is central to the conversation with those who see equality, mercy, compassion, and reconciliation as part and parcel of a meaningful concept of justice and to those who wish to restore justice in our time.

Those who seek greater texture—that moral, spiritual, and aesthetic aspirations be woven into justice—and attend to the local and global grammar of justice and injustice are often referred to as "thick" theorists, while the more positivistic or deontological, rule-governed views of justice tied to specific bodies of laws—most post-Kantian discourse on justice—are often referred to as "thin" theorists.[12] Of course it is the thick views that give us pause and that complicate our analysis of justice! But I am convinced that we must not avoid this more complicated path.

NOTES

1. Stanley Cavell, *In Quest of the Ordinary: Lines of Skepticism and Romanticism* (Chicago: University of Chicago Press, 1988), 21.

2. I owe this last thought to Fergus Kerr, *Immortal Longings: Versions of Transcending Humanity* (London: SPCK, 1997), 164.

3. Robert C. Solomon and Mark C. Murphy, eds., *What Is Justice: Classic and Contemporary Readings,* 2d ed. (New York and Oxford: Oxford University Press, 2000).

4. Michael J. Sandel, *Liberalism and the Limits of Justice*, 2d ed. (Cambridge: Cambridge University Press, 1998), 2. Sandel further says that many liberal thinkers emphasize the importance of justice even while championing the sanctity of "individual rights," 2.

See also Alasdair MacIntyre, *After Virtue: A Study in Moral Theory* (Notre Dame: University of Notre Dame Press, 1981). See especially chapters 17, "Justice as a Virtue: Changing Conceptions," and 18, "After Virtue: Nietzsche *or* Aristotle, Trotsky *and* St. Benedict."

5. Raimond Gaita, *A Common Humanity* (London and New York, Routledge, 2000), 9.

6. See Emmanuel C. Eze, *Achieving Our Humanity* (New York and London: Routledge, 2001). Eze discusses the idea of race and racism that pervades Enlightenment philosophy and that lingers in our current thinking. See especially his chapters 1 and 2.

7. Three principals in this discussion are John Rawls, *A Theory of Justice* (Oxford: Oxford University Press, 1971); Robert Nozick, *Anarchy, State, and Utopia* (Oxford: Basil Blackwell, 1974); and Alasdair MacIntyre, *After Virtue, A Study in Moral Theory* and *Whose Justice? Which Rationality?* (Notre Dame: University of Notre Dame Press, 1988).

Interesting discussions of contemporary views of post-Kantian ideas can be found in Michael Sandel, *Liberalism and the Limits of Justice* (1998) and Onora O'Neill, *Bounds of Justice* (Cambridge: Cambridge University Press, 2000), especially chapters 4 and 5.

8. John Dunn, *Western Political Theory in the Face of the Future*, 2d ed. (Cambridge: Cambridge University Press, 1993), 132.

9. John Dunn, *Western Political Theory in the Face of the Future*, 133.

10. It is not accidental that Simone Weil figures prominently in the background of this book and also as a frame for some particular issues related to understanding the concept of justice. I have written a book on her view of justice and civil society and edited another book dealing with her ideas on the philosophy of culture and politics. See Richard H. Bell, *Simone Weil: The Way of Justice as Compassion* (Rowman & Littlefield Publishers, 1998), and Richard H. Bell, ed. *Simone Weil's Philosophy of Culture* (Cambridge: Cambridge University Press, 1993).

11. In Stephen Mulhall, *Stanley Cavell, Philosophy's Recounting of the Ordinary*, (Oxford: Oxford University Press, 1994), 279.

12. This distinction of "thick and thin theories" has its origins in the writings of social anthropologist and cultural theorist Clifford Geertz. See his *Interpretation of Cultures* (New York: Basic Books, 1973), chapter 1.

This distinction is also made with respect to political theory and justice in Michael Waltzer's *Thick and Thin* (Notre Dame, IN, Notre Dame University Press, 1994). A good example of "thick" analysis of justice in the framework of the pervasive deontological views can also be found in Sandel's *Liberalism and the Limits of Justice*, the "Conclusion" to chapter 4.

Chapter One

The Concept of Justice:
Some Recent Perspectives

When the Berlin Wall came down, when Vaclav Havel stood on the balcony in Prague's Wenceslas Square and crowds cheered the collapse of communist regimes across Europe, I thought, like many people, that we were about to witness a new era of liberal democracy . . .

Now I am not so sure. I began the journey as a liberal, and I end as one, but I cannot help thinking that liberal civilization—the rule of laws, not men, of argument in place of force, of compromise in place of violence— runs deeply against the human grain and is only achieved and sustained by the most unremitting struggle against human nature. The liberal virtues— tolerance, compromise, reason—remain as valuable as ever, but they cannot be preached to those who are mad with fear or mad with vengeance.

[Michael Ignatieff, from his *Blood and Belonging* (1993)]

Justice appears in "that halt, that interval of hesitation, wherein lies all our consideration for our brothers in humanity."

[Simone Weil, *The Iliad: Or the Poem of Force*]

"FACING" OUR HUMANITY:
CONTEXTUALIZING JUSTICE AND INJUSTICE

Much has transpired in the period since the Berlin Wall fell. New democracies have emerged but so, too, have new fears and intolerance. Many share Ignatieff's sentiments about the value of "liberal virtues," but it is not so easy to profess, let alone practice, such virtues without seeing the specific contexts in which they may apply or from which they have vanished or for whom they may be unwelcome guests. Our task is to look hard at the contexts of such

9

virtues and see what should be added or revised to make them hospitable in rethinking the virtue of justice.

Alasdair MacIntyre's book *Whose Justice? Which Rationality?* (1988), is a helpful reminder to reset our thinking about the concept of "justice" and much oppression in the name of justice. Among other things he helps us identify conditions of inequality and oppression in their respective contexts. Today, having two cultures next to each other may particularize the concept of justice in ways that make them unrecognizable to each other. Thus to look at differences in traditions, in rules of law, in religious faiths, particularizes any discussion of the concept of justice and helps us to avoid clichés and abstractions in our use of the concept. This is not, however, to make the concept "justice" simply relative to context. A wrong done—from harming a child to the Holocaust, from sexual abuse to indiscriminate bombing of civilians—is particular to a place, but its "wrongness" is recognizable beyond place. This idea is, of course, found earlier in such philosophers as Socrates and more recently Simone Weil and Ludwig Wittgenstein, among others. Let me elaborate on this point.

Socrates, for example, always drew his readers into focused and very specific conversation. In his dialogues with Crito, Gorgias, Polis, Thrasymachus, or Glaucon, we overhear his views on justice and are forced to reflect on his interlocutors' views as well. In the early dialogues of Plato, Socrates believed that justice was a simple reflection of our full humanity. To be just made all of our moral action toward one another transparent and it was owed to all. In the Crito, Socrates says to his friend: a just person does no harm, he does not retaliate for any reason, he does not render evil for evil. Rush Rhees says that among Socrates' virtues is that he awakens in his interlocutors and his readers through Plato "the sense of what is degrading: or the sense of good and evil."[1] To evoke such a sense requires clear deliberation and understanding of the circumstances of those who are degraded or degrade others. Socrates' views, however, seem to undergo a transformation in Plato's hands as they enter the context of politics and society in *The Republic*. An idea of "three kinds of men" enters into the discussion as we hear Socrates say to Glaucon: "I think we shall say that a man is just in the same way as the city is just. . . . We have surely not forgotten that the city was just because each of the three classes in it was fulfilling its own task." Each of the three classes was given "what is owed to him"—as if some individual or class entitlement view is being inserted. It is as if the notion of justice reflecting our full humanity and something owed "to all" slips into a functional role to maintain the order of the City State. There seems to be two views competing with one another: Socrates' and Plato's. We will look further at these differences later.

Among recent and contemporary philosophers there are stirrings to return to simple certainties understood by Socrates that to do justice is a fundamental expression *of one's humanity*. What appeared commonsensical or a given must now be provided with elaborate reasons for such claims. Such reasons are emerging, however, and once again they return us to some base intuition about what it means to be a human being, on how to be just toward one's fellow citizens or a distant stranger. Several recent studies of justice have given greater attention to ordinary contexts and to the importance of conversation or deliberation. These studies note where the moral and political converge around discussions of justice. Of note are Jonathan Glover's *Humanity: A Moral History of the Twentieth Century*, Raimond Gaita's *A Common Humanity: Thinking about Love and Truth and Justice*, and Elizabeth Wolgast's *The Grammar of Justice*.[2] Wolgast, for example, focuses our attention on context by suggesting that we come to understand justice by recognizing forms of "injustice"—an idea that Aristotle had also suggested. The first line of reasoning in Wolgast is to argue that little sense can be made of the meaning of justice without getting clear on examples of "injustice." She writes: "Instead of fastening our attention on justice the substantive, let us examine some of the contexts where justice is evoked, that is complaints against injustice. In the face of wrong justice is demanded and cried out for, and with passion and intensity. 'We must have justice,' and 'Justice must be done!' are its expressions, and they characteristically have imperative force as well as urgency."[3] To raise such alarm is, as Wolgast says, "to take it out of the realm of disinterested reportage. . . . saying that something is a wrong or injustice *marks it* for moral indignation and moral concern."[4]

This, too, is a characteristic feature of Glover's work as he examines numerous examples of injustice in the past century. In doing so he calls us first "not to look away"[5] from the harmdoing of which we are capable. Furthermore, he asks us to cultivate enough *moral imagination* to overcome distance.[6] Glover provokes our moral imagination with the following brief story:

> In 1985, in the old apartheid South Africa, there was a demonstration in Durban. The police attacked the demonstrators with customary violence. One policeman chased a black woman, obviously intending to beat her with his club. As she ran, her shoe slipped off. The brutal policeman was also a well brought up young Afrikaner, who knew that when a woman loses her shoe you pick it up for her. *Their eyes met* as he handed her the shoe. He then left her, since clubbing her was no longer an option.[7]

Glover then remarks: "This act and the eye-meet together triggered a breakthrough of normal human responses and their tendency to inhibit violence."[8] "For most people, most of the time," says Glover, "the virtues which matter are local and personal. *In ordinary life kindness counts for more than belief in human rights*."[9]

Glover asks us to look at, or "face," injustice wherever and whenever it occurs. The idea of looking at or facing injustice resonates with the more philosophical notion developed by Emmanuel Levinas who argued that the foundation of all ethics is in the idea of alterity, or in being confronted by the face of the other. Levinas is given major credit for helping revive philosophical ethics during the second half of the twentieth century; of rescuing ethics from the positivists and analytic meta-ethical accounts of the 1960s and 1970s where virtually all "local and personal" or "ordinary" moral acts were displaced by abstract ethical theory. "Ethics begins," says Levinas, "before the exteriority of the *other*, before other people, and, as I like to put it, before the face of the other, which engages my responsibility by its human expression."[10] It is as I "look at" or "regard" the other, Levinas says, that "the other *concerns* me."[11]

There is for Levinas priority to the face of the other by virtue of my having once treated the other badly or unjustly, or by virtue of my being in the place of the other. He says:

> One has to respond to one's right to be, not by referring to some abstract and anonymous law, or judicial entity, but because of one's fear for the Other. My being-in-the-world or my "place in the sun," my being at home, have these not also been the usurpation of spaces belonging to the other man whom I have already oppressed or starved, or driven out into a third world; are they not acts of repulsing, excluding, exiling, stripping, killing? Pascal's "my place in the sun" marks the beginning of the image of the usurpation of the whole earth.[12]

Thus, I define my humanity by how I face the other, by what Levinas says is my "proximity" to the other. "The Other becomes my neighbor precisely through the way the face summons me, calls for me, begs for me, and in so doing recalls my responsibility, and calls me into question."[13] Any indifference to the other subverts my humanity. Ethics, then, has its foundation in my proximity to the other, the stranger, my neighbor, the one nearest to me, and this proximity is a response that requires that I give up my ego and its sovereignty and accept responsibility for the other. The priority here forms an obligation for the other before I can claim any "right." Therein lies my humanity. Levinas puts it this way: "It is in the laying down by the ego of its sovereignty (in its 'hateful' modality), that we find ethics and also probably the very spirituality of the soul, but most certainly the question of the meaning of being."[14] In another context he noted: "to see a face is already to hear 'you shall not kill,' and to hear 'you shall not kill' is to hear 'Social justice.'"[15]

This idea that ethics begins when you look into the face of another is also an important notion in thinking about what it is in our actions that makes us human; that constitutes our humanity. Wittgenstein—like Levinas, although a few decades earlier—also taught us that being a human being is caught up in the very fabric of relating to others. He says that what meaning we give to our life is in the manner that we approach others. It is as if at some point in our long human history we suddenly realized that who I am as a human being is tied to others like me, and that I must interact with them in a mutually interested way. The meaning of myself is tied to others in a mysterious manner. He says simply, "meaning something is like going up to someone."[16] And in another place he describes our mutual recognition of our humanity as "an attitude toward a soul."[17] This is not some metaphysical pronouncement linked to the "mind-body" problem he is evoking here, but the depth of the mutual recognition of the needs and wants of humans and the trust needed to mutually fulfill those needs and wants. *It could be argued that the concept of justice is, in part, a reflection of this kind of reciprocal acknowledgment of the humanness of the other whenever and wherever you "go up to them."* This is not to say that everyone we meet will be embraced as a "friend" or "lover"—but even a "stranger" or an "enemy" will evoke meaning in the manner of the encounter and the encounter should include some form of an attitude toward a soul—a recognized quality of being human. Perhaps it is even "the very spirituality of the soul" as Levinas said. In the case of a stranger or an enemy there will be degrees of hesitation, consideration, caution, perhaps fear or enmity. All that surrounds our mutual encounters with others play a part in our moral practices toward them, and *being just* toward one another is the highest of those practices. The Greek word we translate into English for the practice of justice is *dikaiosune* or "being righteous."

Reflecting a similar idea—an idea Simone Weil calls "reading" another human being, she writes:

> Anybody who is in our vicinity exercises a certain power over us by his very presence, and a power that belongs to him alone, that is, the power of halting, repressing, modifying each movement that our body sketches out. If we step aside for a passer-by on the road, it is not the same thing as stepping aside to avoid a bill-board; alone in our rooms, we get up, walk about, sit down again quite differently from the way we do when we have a visitor. . . .[18]
>
> [And in another essay she writes:] Acting either on oneself or on another consists in transforming meanings. A man, the head of state, declares war, and new meanings spring up around each of forty million men. . . .War, politics, rhetoric, art, education, every action directed towards others consists essentially in changing what men read [i.e. how we "go up to someone."][19]

Beyond "facing," or "going up to," or "reading" the other, Glover undertakes a "genealogy" of the morality of the twentieth century—a century often thought to be especially good at reinventing cruelty—where he gives us revealing accounts of "face" encounters between humans during times of tension, war, genocide, the Holocaust, and more. He further argues that justice requires that we not look away from the cruelty or evil but be mindful of it and find ways to help us restore a sense of justice. His focus is on the complex qualities in our humanity that surface in the face of cruelty and that allow us to engage in everyday acts of kindness and to consider justice as connected to sympathy and compassion.

On Glover's point of cultivating our moral imagination, Simone Weil is both provocative and prescient. In unconventional ways and extraordinary use of ordinary concepts, she juxtaposes injustice and justice, harmdoing, and compassion. This brings a new sense to the notion of justice into focus—or we might say "an older sense of justice" takes on new life for our time. In all these encounters between humans where we define the meaning of our lives, the most important movement with respect to justice is what she calls "that halt, that interval of hesitation, wherein lies all our consideration for our brothers in humanity."[20] This she also calls in numerous contexts: attention. She even says that developing "the power of attention in children, by school exercises to be sure, but [also] by reminding them ceaselessly that they must be attentive in order to be able, later on, to be just."[21]

CLASSICAL CONCEPTIONS OF JUSTICE

Let us back up for a moment to look at the shaping of the philosophical concept of justice in early Greek thought. In *Homer*, the word *dike*—justice in the conceptual sense—acts in a corrective sense to an individual who would abrogate custom and mores. Justice [*dike*] was an action of a kind that "restored" the social order; that worked to balance grievances with both a social and moral overtone. In this period, Martha Nussbaum notes, "the world of strict *dike* is a harsh and symmetrical world in which order and design are preserved with exceptionless clarity."[22] Even though Homer's great epic poems were wrought with grievances and reprisals, there were periodic moments of hesitation—moments of reflection or even more formal deliberations in an *agora*, an assembly called where all citizens could speak—that might lead to the settling of grievances. It may be true that part of the "corrective" justice in the *Iliad* is played out in retaliation or revenge, but a parallel subtext is the anguish and suffering that follows such actions of revenge. This is what Simone Weil saw as the heart of "justice" in the face of "injustices." She believed that the poem was "bathed in justice and love" with regard to an individual's sense of anguish, suffering and compassion. She said in her essay on the *Iliad*, "Justice and love, which hardly have any place in this study of extremes and unjust acts of violence, nevertheless bathe the work in their light without ever becoming noticeable themselves, except as a kind of accent."[23] So we see two faces of justice: first, its more formal judicial sense, played out either through taking revenge or through a procedure in the *agora* and a search for some sort of balance of power, and second, its sense of restoration of peace or cessation of violence through compassion and love—even forgiveness.

The principles that can be gleaned from the more formal procedures are deliberation (civic debate), balance of power or restoration of order, and some sort of social or communal reconciliation. Whereas, in modern theories of justice individuation is the engine that controls or drives what we call civic-order. Classicist Erik Havelock notes that in early Greek conceptions of justice "such procedures may have been . . . invented to control the impact of individuation upon nascent human communities."[24] Moving from Homer's *Iliad*, Havelock looks at the development of the idea of justice in the *Odyssey*, in Solon, the pre-Socratic philosophers, and in Aeschylus before arriving at Plato. Some of his ideas need mentioning. He notes that, for example, "the just man of the *Odyssey* showed his quality by his treatment of the traveling stranger, and also of the poor and destitute; what he should grant them is equity."[25]

Solon is believed to be the first to articulate both a procedure and a polity with respect to the meaning of justice. Havelock says that Solon is "the first statesman on the [Western] scene, through his program of impartial protection for rich and poor, noble and commoner, powerful and powerless."[26] He sees justice as equity. He gets this partly from the *Iliad* and the *Odyssey*. Part of the difficulty in seeing Solon's views clearly is that although he is known as "the lawgiver" his legal codes did not survive in written texts and must be pieced together through fragments of his poetry and secondary references.

A clearer concept of justice seems to be taking hold by the mid-sixth century (BCE) Athenian state. Aeschylus, in his *Oresteia* trilogy, tries to stem the cycle of vengeance. Havelock says,

> one of the most powerful impressions conveyed by the *Oresteia* is that of human beings caught in the web of continuous crime from which they cannot escape. Yet escape occurs. . . . The *Eumenides* (the third in the trilogy) devotes itself to dramatizing the way in which this might take place. The solution is to create an institution—it is actually on stage—namely, a court of legality in which [the cycle of] murder and counter murder are replaced by verbal argument from the contending parties and by judicial decision, implemented by the vote of a jury. Shall the most recent perpetrator of murder [Orestes] be destroyed in his turn? By the narrowest of decisions, the vote is no; the series can end.[27]

We have here a formal deliberative procedure, similar to the justice in the *agora* of the *Iliad*. What was earlier seen as a series of reciprocal acts of violence is halted by a just process. Finally, what is needed concludes Havelock, "is reciprocal accommodation, not reciprocal murder."[28]

In the *Oresteia,* as it was earlier conceived in Solon's justice, the "justice" of "retribution"—of reciprocal murder—is transformed to the "justice of civil order in a peaceful and prosperous Athens."[29] Justice of a "civil order" is important here. This idea imbeds justice into the polis and turns over part of the responsibility for justice to the community. Justice becomes the propriety of the reasoned deliberation of the citizens of the state to maintain order. Contemporary philosopher A. C. Grayling underscores this with this assessment of Aeschylus' *Oresteia:*

> The birth of the idea of civil society in the West is recorded by Aeschylus in the third part of his Oresteian trilogy. It tells of Orestes, pursued by the avenging Furies for killing his mother, is rescued by Athene, who offers him a trial by jury in her city of Athens. Revenge had been the cruel justice of the warrior age. Jury trial was the civilized justice of the new, thoughtful age which—despite having a long way to go in such respects as slavery and the rights of women—was then dawning. Aeschylus saw that if citizens had a share in making their society function, society would inevitably be more responsive to their needs and interests.[30]

On the one hand early Greek justice, as poetically rendered, from Homer through Aeschylus, has a strain of retribution, while on the other hand it focuses on the internal moral dilemmas of individual subjects, of suffering and the conflicted lives of human beings. Finally, these two opposing notions are resolved in the frame of civic order, in a human community that sees the importance of human peace and order over violence and revenge. We have, finally, in Plato a written attempt at formalizing the concept of justice within the Greek City State.

Plato is intent on fixing an idea of justice for his City, says Havelock, in order to prevent "justice from slipping through [the thicket] and disappearing."[31] He argues that the most essential ingredient in colonizing the city "is justice." Furthermore, what justice *is,* is for every citizen to "do one's own thing when it occurs in a certain mode"[32]—the mode being as one finds their respective place or role in the City. Thus, in addition to one individually cultivating virtues of temperance, courage and wisdom, what remains is to act justly in order for the Polis to function well. When justice is "present in child, woman, slave, freeman, craftsman, ruler, and ruled," respective to their "modes," then "that will most likely make a good city."[33]

Havelock rightly raises the question: So what does it mean "to do one's own thing (or things)?" This is surely different from our current "parlance" that encourages each person "to do their own thing," thus making one's values and actions relative to fit personal whims and preferences. Here is where the phrase "in a certain mode" is crucial and where Plato's tripartite division of classes comes into the picture. Although this division appeals to the traditional ethic of Greek culture it seems to overlook a crucial issue that Plato had earlier attributed to Socrates. We noted that Socrates clearly made "being just" normative for every person, and this meant doing *no one* harm, nor returning evil for evil—a clear rebuke to retribution. In earlier dialogues, Plato had implied that there is a concept of justice that fits *all* humanity, or at least "all" who would live in an ordered and peaceable City State.

In the *Republic*, however, the view of justice seems to focus on political ends, "on the conservation of existing distributions of property and power, definable only in terms of the status quo."[34] But what of the idea of personal justice? What do we make of the expectation that all human beings must act justly? This was the question uppermost in earlier dialogues. In the *Republic* it appears that Plato has turned away from his principled chief protagonist (Socrates) of the *Apology, Crito,* and *Gorgias,* and imposed a more conservative and traditionalist's view of justice into "Socrates' voice." Justice slips from a mode of personal moral action to one of preserving the existing political order. On the matter of personal justice we read from the *Republic* the following:

> In reality justice pertains not to the outward action (performed) upon one's (concerns), but to the inner, that which really pertains to oneself and to the self's concerns; the individual avoids allowing the elements [*gene*] in the soul to mind each other's business and get involved with each other: he actually makes a proper disposition of (what is) personal to him (*oikeia*): he personally assumes command of and organizes himself [*auton hautou*] and becomes friends to himself. . . becoming in all respects one out of many. . . .[35]

This allows the personal and political understanding of justice to mesh with one another—one "minds one's own business," as we say. It also challenges the ideal of universal human dignity held to be sacred by many as central to the heart of justice. With all the rich and textured features emerging from Homer to Plato, these last moves by Plato are disappointing. In the end, the *Republic* lends itself to some mis-readings of possible hierarchical civil states. Were one to dwell on Homer, Solon, Aeschylus, and Socrates of the earlier dialogues, the possibilities for a highly textured concept of justice that appeals to both personal moral and community political virtues is hopeful. These Greek epic poems, tragedies, and dialogues are fertile for pushing the imagination toward a radical rethinking of justice for our present time; they provide us with a vocabulary and a certain grammar for the use of the concept of justice that merit our attention.

Martha Nussbaum carries our story of antiquity several centuries further to critique the idea of justice as it develops in Aristotle and in Roman thinkers, particularly in Seneca. In her essay "Equity and Mercy," Nussbaum traces the idea of what she calls "situational judgment" in response to a just or unjust act, or "the ability to judge in such a way as to respond with sensitivity to all the particulars of a person and situation and the 'inclination of the mind' to leniency in punishment—equity and mercy."[36] This, I believe, is not unlike our having identified earlier from the *Iliad* "that halt, that interval of hesitation, wherein lies all our consideration for our brothers in humanity," where we pause and measure the circumstances of harm and help. This notion, Nussbaum clearly notes, contrasts with the Greek notion of symmetrical retribution as a way of settling accounts. The concern with particulars—or the equity and mercy tradition—says Nussbaum, "is connected with taking up a gentle and lenient cast of mind toward human wrongdoing."[37] She continues, "*Epieikeia* [equity or mercy] is a gentle art of particular perception, a temper of mind that refuses to demand retribution without understanding the whole story."[38] It was Aristotle in his *Nicomachean Ethics*, argues Nussbaum, who made the first major contribution to combine the equitable with the strict retributive account of justice. She says of Aristotle that his understanding of the *epiekes* "is neither strictly the same as the just nor altogether different in kind." She then goes on:

> Aristotle's solution to the dilemma is that equity is a kind of justice, but a kind . . . opposed to another sort, namely, strict legal justice. It may be regarded as a "correcting" and "completing" of legal justice.
>
> [And Nussbaum continues] Equity . . . acknowledges the terrible dilemmas faced by characters such as Agamemnon, Antigone, and Creon, the terrible badness of all their options. Recognizing the burden of these "human things," the equitable judge is inclined not to be "zealous for strict judgment in the direction of the worse" but to prefer merciful mitigation.[39]

This idea of equity and mercy as worked out by Aristotle becomes a standard feature, suggests Nussbaum, in the Roman philosopher Seneca. Seneca embraces the notion that justice must "examine thoroughly the circumstances of human life." Nussbaum summarizes Seneca's view in the following paragraph:

> Seneca now uses this view as the basis for his argument against retributive anger and in favor of mercy. Given the omnipresence of aggression and wrongdoing, he now argues, if we look at the lives of others with the attitudes typical of the retributive tradition of justice . . . then we will never cease to be retributive and to inflict punishment, for everything we see will upset us. *But this retributive attitude, even when in some sense justified, is not without its consequences for the human spirit. . . . Retributive anger hardens the spirit, turning it against the*

humanity it sees. And in turning against humanity, in evincing the rage and hardness of the angry, one then becomes perilously close to the callous wrongdoers who arouse rage in the first place.[40]

[Finally, Nussbaum narrates Seneca's famous counterproposal, announced at the end of *On Anger*.] We should "cultivate humanity." It is this attitude that he now calls by the name of mercy—translating Greek *epieikeia* with the Latin word *clementia*. . . . [H]e makes a sympathetic participatory attitude central to the norm of good judging. Senecan *clementia* does not fail to pass judgment on wrongdoing; this is continually stressed. *Seneca does not hold that the circumstances of human life remove moral and legal responsibility for bad acts.* We may still convict defendants who fulfill some basic condition of rationality in action. But, looking at the circumstances of human life, one comes to understand how such things have happened. And this . . . understanding leads to mercy.[41]

As can be seen, the Greek and Roman idea of justice from Homer to Seneca is a highly nuanced one. Within it we find most of the concepts familiar to us in thinking about justice and civil society. Some notable features, however, like "attention to circumstances," "community deliberation," "mercy," "compassion," and "equity" seem to have faded from our "modern" more strictly legalistic views.

JUSTICE, POWER, AND RIGHTS

In a line from her essay "*The Iliad*" Simone Weil illustrates this triumph of peace and order over violence and revenge and carries this early Greek idea of justice into our contemporary discussion. She also confirms the Senecan notion that we should pay close attention to "the circumstances of human life" so that we do not harden the human spirit. She says: "Only he who has measured the dominion of force, and knows how *not* to respect it, is capable of love and justice."[42] When I first read this remark, some twenty-five years ago, I remembered the quote without the "not" in it. This accorded in my mind with the *realpolitik* notions that those in power will do all they can to retain their power and that we need to be cognizant of that fact—perhaps not accept this idea of justice, but recognize its currency. But her "not"— learning how not to respect force—leapt out at me at my next reading of the same passage. It woke me from my slumber. She was saying two things here: (a) examine power—those "dominions of force" in our world and how they cause harm to human beings, and (b) learn how *not to* respect power so you will continually struggle with and work toward the elimination of harm. This is the path toward justice. Do not let domains of force control your life; show a *dis*respect for power, only then will you be capable of love and justice.

Here she is working on neutralizing the power of the word "power"—or the concept "the dominion of force"—to show it to be empty with respect to love and justice. What challenges the moral imagination here is the expectation built into us that it is through a kind of Hobbesian power that we control our lives, our social institutions, and our nation states. Each of which she says we should carefully "measure." In the essay "The *Iliad*" she appeals to our imagination through the poetic force of this epic—an epic that she says on the one hand defines the very concept of power, while on the other hand is indirectly "bathed" in the concepts of "justice and love."

Simone Weil explores this idea further in her hermeneutical essay "The Power of Words." Because she knows, like the Greeks knew, that those who wield power—those who know how to use the word "power" and deploy its meaning—will either "command our respect" or seek to neutralize us or "destroy us." If, however, we learn to understand, or "measure," the word, we will come to know how *not* to respect it. She says that "when a word is properly defined it loses its capital letters and can no longer serve either as a banner or as a hostile slogan. . . ." In clarifying our thought about "power" and its harmfulness, "strange though it may appear," we might find "a way of saving human lives."[43] Imagine saying such a thing—that attention to words may save lives! Once such a radical notion as "understand the word" and it "may save lives" is expressed she goes on to talk about our politicians' use of such words as patriotism (as in the American "patriot act"), national security, property, order, democracy, capitalism, communism, fascism, terrorism. Having evoked such examples in our imagination she goes on to say: "Each of these words seem to represent for us an absolute reality, unaffected by conditions, or an absolute objective, independent of methods of action, or an absolute evil; and at the same time we make all these words mean, successively or simultaneously, anything whatsoever."[44] Her point is that if we see these words in their proper use contexts, stripped of abstraction—or as she says stripped "of their capital letters"—and look at them at ground level, they may be modified and used without abuse or danger.

Following her concern over the meaning of words, Simone Weil provides us with a compelling look at how the concept of "rights" in modern Western legal circles has virtually displaced a meaningful concept of "justice."[45] This is partly due to the rise of the idea from Thomas Hobbes to Robert Nozick of the "social contract" as the foundation for law. The social contract is seen to be a matter between individuals—to promising and keeping promises and to making a "contract." Our rush to preserve individual rights leads to our "forgetting" the community or that justice is to serve our full humanity. There is no longer any meaning to the idea of the "social" in social contract, only "*my* right to . . ." in spite of the fact that such individual detachment from one's social setting is unattainable. As Luce Irigaray, in her provocative *Democracy Begins Between Two*, says: "Indeed, society is not made up of one + one + one neutral and separate individuals, but of individuals who are linked together."[46] Numerous other women [and men] philosophers—Martha Nussbaum, Catherine MacKinnon, Annette Baier, Nel Noddings, and others espousing more communitarian views—have joined in a chorus to remind us of the fabric of the social, of gendered relations and relations of mother and child, husband and wife, of power relations of employer/employee, oppressor and oppressed.

Furthermore, if justice is reduced to the protection of individual rights and subsequent litigation to "get one's due" when rights are violated, we lose a necessary fabric of justice that underlies human relationships—respect for another's dignity. Does not a "society" assume that we treat strangers as fellow citizens with some respect as well as those with whom we are most closely related? Simone Weil gives us the striking example of a young girl "forced into a brothel" and contends, "she had great harm done to her which cannot be understood as a 'right' taken." In fact she goes on, "if a young girl is being forced into a brothel she will not talk about her rights. In such a situation the word would sound ludicrously inadequate."[47] Weil is clear that "justice . . . has lost its meaning and been replaced by a 'vacuous' notion of 'rights' which 'makes us forget the value of life." She understands the obsession with rights as transforming "what should have been a cry of protest from the depths of the heart [or from some respect for the value of life] into a shrill nagging of claims and counter-claims [a "he did . . . she did" battle] which is both impure and unpractical."[48]

In many modern moral and political views individual liberties are given the highest priority. This requires a long list of "rights" that are not to be interfered with. "Rights" talk is gradually taken out of its moral context and drifts toward a legalistic context—or, at least, what we call "rights" becomes a morally neutral notion. As a morally neutral notion, rights carry no positive obligations. For example, if a friend is being mugged, I may believe it is the right course of action, morally, to intervene and prevent or stop the mugging. But on a "rights-based" view, for example, moral ambiguity creeps in. There is no intrinsic "right" that a person be helped, and there is no positive "right" that obligates me to help.[49] Or if I see poverty, I am under no obligation to be generous. And because my notion of a good or a life-plan may be different from yours and everyone else's goods and plans, I am in no way compelled to agree with your course of action. I may criticize your good and your plan, but I will be inclined to choose not to interfere so that I do not invite your interference with my good and plan. It becomes an easy slide into moral relativism or moral neutrality. The possibility of moral consensus or a common good diminishes as individualism increases, and the stake I may have in protecting my good from another's goes up as my moral concern decreases.

OBLIGATIONS AND RECIPROCITY

Simone Weil has a clear way of shifting this slide to moral neutrality. The opening sentence in *The Need for Roots* reads: "The notion of obligation takes precedence over that of rights, which is subordinate and relative to it."[50] J. P. Little, in *Simone Weil: Waiting on Truth*, says that in this one sentence Simone Weil "dispenses with several centuries of thinking on the fundamental principles of social organization, including, of course, all the national and international charters for the protection of human freedoms from the American Declaration of Independence and the French Revolutionary Declaration of Human Rights onwards." Little goes on to show how in *The Need for Roots* Simone Weil criticizes "rights" on two grounds:

> firstly, a right is worthless except in conjunction with its corresponding obligation; it is of no use to me to have rights if no one else recognizes them. Secondly, and more importantly in Simone Weil's eyes, rights belong to an inferior order, and are always conditioned by particular circumstances. The notion of rights is a legal one (in French *le droit* means both "right" and "the law"), and is linked to that of quantity, exchange, property.

On the other hand, moving from rights to justice, Weil says:

> Justice is based on mutual consent, and the cry of someone suffering injustice is "Why am I being hurt?" The notion of rights, being based on property, produces a different cry: "Why has he got more than I have?" (EL 38). The notion of obligation is unconditional, since it is situated on a higher plane than that of rights; the only difficulty lies in grasping the theoretical basis for the obligation towards one's fellow-beings, and then finding practical expression for it.[51]

Little finds the theoretical basis for obligation in the "Draft for a Statement of Human Obligations," written at the same time as *The Need for Roots*. In the "Draft," Simone Weil writes:

> Whoever has his attention and love turned in fact towards that reality outside the world recognizes at the same time that he is bound, in both public and private life, by the unique and perpetual obligation, according to his responsibilities and to the extent of his power, to alleviate all those privations of the soul and the

body capable of destroying or mutilating the earthly life of a human being whoever he may be.[52]

Simone Weil's idea of a "reality outside the world" simply places the idea of justice on a higher plane than that of rights; justice is not relative to our individual wants, or as she said to that of "quantity, exchange, property." We have earlier in this chapter also sketched out an ontological foundation for the priority of the notion of obligation or responsibility for the other in our discussions of Levinas, Glover, and Wittgenstein.

More recently, Annette Baier suggests that the idea of social contract can be salvaged partially from its atomistic nature—from its overemphasis on individuation of rights—by introducing the concept of "trust" into the public discourse on justice. She considers trust or "reliance on another's good will"—a form of some mutual respect—to be as pervasive among human interactions as air is to the atmosphere. With such mutual respect goes a sense of reciprocity and obligation. When trust breaks down the human social fabric deteriorates.[53] On this last point Onora O'Neill has focused attention on the connection between rights and obligations in the matter of trust—a point she acknowledges was earlier central to Simone Weil's idea of justice. O'Neill says: "If duties (or *obligations*) *are prior to rights* we need to reorient our political thinking."[54]

O'Neill criticizes the United Nations Declaration of Human Rights because it says almost nothing about duties or obligations. It is only if citizens accept obligations that one another's rights can be secured. O'Neill begins "with the Kantian thought that we are all moral equals . . . for Kant the deeper implication is that we all have equal duties. No competent person, and none of the institutions that human beings construct, is exempt from fundamental duties. The basic principles of justice—like all ethical principles—are *principles for all*. We should not therefore act on principles that are unfit to be principles for all."[55] In haste to affirm individual rights, this basic principle of justice is often forgotten, even among many contemporary Kantians. O'Neill concludes:

If we think rights are the *preconditions* of social and political trust, there is nothing *we* can do until *other* people start respecting *our* rights—and nothing *they* can do until *we* start respecting *their* rights. If we persist in taking a passive view of human beings seeing them primarily as holders of rights and forgetting that those rights are the flip side of others' duties, restoring trust may seem a hopeless task. But if we remember that human beings must act before *anyone* can have rights there is a different way of looking at matters. Some duties that support trust can be met even in the darkest times.[56]

Also linked with the idea of mutual trust being necessary for justice, Luce Irigaray refers to the relationship between two loving people as ideally involving "an ability to relate to the self in order to perceive and contemplate who the other is, and also to be able to feel oneself as oneself. . . ."[57] Irigaray is here concerned with the sensation of empathy (or sympathetic understanding) and the consequences of internalizing the anguish of another. The same meaning can be applied to "pity," "love," "trust," and a myriad of other human aspirations purported to be inextricable from a satisfactory account of what it means to be just. When such human inclinations fail us or cease, injustice easily surfaces.

These concerns of trust and obligation, reciprocity and self-identity are developed in their purest form in Simone Weil's account of friendship. Weil writes:

> Friendship has something universal about it. It consists of loving a human being as we should like to be able to love each soul in particular of all those who go to make up the human race. . . . The consent to preserve an autonomy within ourselves and in others is essentially of a universal order.
>
> There is not friendship where distance is not kept and respected . . . . Pure friendship is rare.[58]

Friendship allows each person in the relationship his or her complete autonomy. You cannot either "wish to please or . . . desire to dominate" a friend: "In a perfect friendship these two desires are completely absent. The two friends have fully consented to be two and not one, they respect the distance which the fact of being two distinct creatures places between them."[59] The goal of friendship is to establish a bond of affection and respect with another human being without any degree of necessity—you love one another without needing one another or expecting anything from the other, or not desiring the other. A friendship is sustained because "each wished to preserve the faculty of free consent both in himself and in the other."[60] This is a picture of an ideal and purely just relationship between two. The practicalities of extending such a relationship as a community grows, as cultures differ, as politics collide, complicate the orders of justice. Formulas for getting along peaceably, maintaining equality and liberty when powers dominate, cultures clash, and conversation diminishes. This, of course is why justice requires vigilance, patience, and deliberation as well as those human qualities of trust, friendship, equity, mercy, love, and compassion. With these concepts in mind the pure rationality proffered by the Enlightenment seems woefully inadequate to the task of achieving justice.

It should be clear from what we have been arguing that a robust ("thick") concept of justice requires a full range of human emotions and aspirations found in the lives of individuals as well as an idea of community or social order that enables reciprocity and cooperation between human beings wherein they can realize their full humanity. This requires what Simone Weil calls a "change in the direction of justice." As long as we are in the grip of vacuous "rights talk" and wedded primarily to the idea of the individual in our understanding of "social" contract, we will never move in the direction of justice.

We have seen that one way in which justice has been diminished in our Enlightenment culture is by reducing it to rights discourse—a thin concept of justice at best. A change in the direction of a more meaningful concept of justice would entail that we not ignore the human condition where people cry out for the injustices done to them and that we pay attention to the affliction suffered from the injustice. What arises from the kind of unconditional attention to the afflicted is some sense of obligation to the other. It is only when one comes "face to face with one's neighbor," as Vaclav Havel has said, that the human heart can be opened and responsibility in love can be exercised.[61] A just person never turns a deaf ear to a particular injustice done to a particular human being. The attention that a culture and justice demand draws goodness into the world through individual acts of kindness and love even in the darkest times.

Current moral philosophy is taking on some heartening new directions, especially as it reexamines moral and social virtues like "justice." In addition to its turn toward what is called "virtue ethics" and the revival of important "accents" from more ancient views of justice, moral philosophy is taking more seriously actual contexts *of injustice and human cruelty*. It asks if mercy should be considered as part of legal justice, and whether "rights" language should be augmented with concepts such as obligation and trust, friendship and compassion in thinking about justice. In this same spirit, Martha Nussbaum asks us two questions in her introduction to *Sex and Social Justice*: "How should we think about each other across the divisions that a legacy of injustice has created? How—given the ample grounds history gives people for suspicion, anger, and even perhaps hatred—might we overcome hatred by love?"[62] Once again the terms "injustice," "good," "evil," and "love" enter the discussion of justice.

NOTES

1. Rush Rhees, *Discussions of Simone Weil*, ed. D. Z. Phillips, asst. Mario von der Ruhr (Albany: State University of New York Press, 1999), 82.

2. Philip P. Hallie earlier pioneered this more focused contextual-historical approach to contemporary ethics by looking at human moral issues through the lenses of cases of "good and evil." See his *Lest Innocent Blood Be Shed: The Story of the*

Village of Le Chambon and How Goodness Happened There (San Francisco: Harper & Row, 1979) and *In the Eye of the Hurricane: Tales of Good and Evil, Help and Harm* (New York: HarperCollins Publishers, 1997). We will draw some examples from these works later.

3. Elizabeth Wolgast, *The Grammar of Justice* (Ithaca: Cornell University Press, 1987), 128.

4. Wolgast, *The Grammar of Justice*, 203.

5. Glover, *Humanity: A Moral History of the Twentieth Century* (New Haven and London: Yale University Press, 2001), 406.

6. Glover, *Humanity,* 409f.

7. Glover, *Humanity*, 37f. My emphasis. Glover notes: "I am grateful to David Spurrett, an eye-witness, for this account."

8. Glover, *Humanity*, 38.

9. Glover, *Humanity,* 41. My emphasis. We shall discuss the contrast between understanding "rights," as in "human rights," with understanding "justice" in a subsequent chapter.

10. Emanuel Levinas, "Martin Buber, Gabriel Marcel and Philosophy," in *Outside the Subject* (London: The Athlone Press, 1993), 35.

11. Levinas, "The Rights of Man and the Rights of the Other," in *Outside the Subject*, 124 and note 3, 167. Levinas further comments: "Should not the fraternity that is in the motto of the [French] republic be discerned in the prior non-indifference of one for the other, in that original goodness in which freedom is embedded, and in which the justice of the rights of man takes on an immutable significance and stability, better than those guaranteed by the state?" 125.

12. Emmanuel Levinas, "Ethics as First Philosophy," in *The Levinas Reader*, ed. Sean Hand (Oxford: Basil Blackwell, 1989), 82.

13. Levinas, *The Levinas Reader*, 83.

14. Levinas, *The Levinas Reader*, 85.

15. Levinas, *Difficult Freedom: Essays on Judaism*, trans. Sean Hand (Baltimore: Johns Hopkins University Press, 1990), 8, 9.

16. Ludwig Wittgenstein, *Philosophical Investigations* (London: The Macmillan Co., 1953), Part I, Sections 455, 457, 132f.

17. Wittgenstein, *Philosophical Investigations*, Part II, iv.178.

18. Simone Weil, *The Iliad or The Poem of Force*, trans. Mary McCarthy (Wallingford, PA: Pendle Hill Pamphlet, no. 91, 1981), 7.

19. Simone Weil, "Essay on the Notion of Reading," trans. Rebecca Fine Rose and Timothy Tessin. *Philosophical Investigations* 13:4 (October 1990, 302). Originally published as "Essay sur la notion de lecture." *Etude Philosophiques* (Marseilles), N.S. 1 (January–March 1946): 13–16.

20. Simone Weil, *The Iliad*, 14.

21. See both her essay *London Fragments* of 1942–1943 and her essay "On the Right Use of School Studies with a View to the Love of God," in *Waiting for God*, trans. Emma Craufurd (New York: Harper Colophon Books, 1951).

22. Martha Nussbaum, *Sex and Social Justice* (Oxford: Oxford University Press, 1999), 159.

23. Simone Weil, *Iliad*, 30.

24. Eric A. Havelock, *The Greek Concept of Justice: From Its Shadows in Homer to Its Substance in Plato* (Cambridge, MA, and London: Harvard University Press, 1978), 137.

25. Havelock, *The Greek Concept of Justice*, 255.

26. Havelock, *The Greek Concept of Justice*, 254f.

27. Havelock, *The Greek Concept of Justice*, 279.

28. Havelock, *The Greek Concept of Justice*, 280.

29. Havelock, *The Greek Concept of Justice*, 287.

30. A. C. Grayling, op ed *The Times Weekend Review*, March 13, 2004, 9. It is interesting that this comment on the *Oresteia* comes in an editorial concerned with how contemporary imperial powers, namely Great Britain and the United States, are engaged in an "avenging war," and seem to have lost sight of deliberation.

31. Havelock, *The Greek Concept of Justice*, 316.

32. Havelock, *The Greek Concept of Justice*, 317.

33. Havelock, *The Greek Concept of Justice*, 318.

34. Havelock, *The Greek Concept of Justice*, 320.

35. Havelock, *The Greek Concept of Justice*, 322.

36. Martha C. Nussbaum, *Sex and Social Justice* (Oxford: Oxford University Press, 1999), 156.

37. Nussbaum, *Sex and Social Justice*, 156.

38. Nussbaum, *Sex and Social Justice*, 159.

39. Nussbaum, *Sex and Social Justice*, 160, 161.

40. Nussbaum, *Sex and Social Justice*, 165. My emphasis.

41. Nussbaum, *Sex and Social Justice*, 166. My emphasis.

42. Simone Weil, *Iliad*, 34. My emphasis.

43. Simone Weil, "The Power of Words," in *Selected Essays: 1934–1943*, trans. Richard Rees (Oxford: Oxford University Press, 1962), 156.

44. Simone Weil, "The Power of Words," 157.

45. See her essay "Human Personality" in *Selected Essays: 1934–1943*. *Passim.*

46. Luce Irigaray, *Democracy Begins Between Two*, trans Kirsteen Anderson (New York: Routledge, 2001), 118.

47. Simone Weil, *Selected Essays*, 21.

48. I have discussed this point about "rights" and "justice" at length in my book *Simone Weil: The Way of Justice as Compassion* (Lanham, MD: Rowman & Littlefield Publishers, 1998). See especially chapter 3, 38–46.

49. There are exceptions to this. Curiously in French law, unlike U.S. and British law, this is qualified by what is sometimes called a "good Samaritan" law which says that if you come upon a person in danger, and you have the skills to help (you are a doctor, strong swimmer, etc.), you are obliged to help. If you can help and do not, you risk both social approbrium and legal sanctions. Simone Weil would understand this as a point in law and social order that moves in the direction of justice. This point was brought to my attention by Christine Ann Evans.

50. Simone Weil, *The Need for Roots*, trans. Arthur Wills with a preface by T. S. Eliot (New York: Harper Colophon Books, 1971), 3.

51. J. P. Little, *Simone Weil: Waiting on Truth,* Berg Women's Series (Oxford: St. Martin's Press, 1988), 85.

52. Simone Weil, *Selected Essays*, 222, trans. J. P. Little. More will be said about this notion of "reality outside the world" in our last chapter on "justice and spirituality."

53. Annette Baier, "Against Social Contract Understanding of Justice," from "Trust and Antitrust," as found in *What Is Justice?* eds. Solomon and Murphy, 121.

54. Onora O'Neill, *A Question of Trust* (Cambridge: Cambridge University Press, 2002), 31.

55. O'Neill, *A Question of Trust*, 31–33.

56. O'Neill, *A Question of Trust*, 35.

57. Luce Irigary, *Democracy Begins Between Two* (New York: Routledge, 2001), 111.

58. Simone Weil, *Waiting for God*, 206f.

59. Simone Weil, *Waiting for God*, 205.

60. Simone Weil, *Waiting for God*. 204.

61. See Havel's *Letters to Olga* (New York: Henry Holt and Company, 1989), 370f. A larger discussion of Havel's views on "facing one's neighbor" and "responsibility and justice" can be found later in chapter seven.

62. Martha Nussbaum, *Sex and Social Justice*, 5.

Chapter Two

Justice: Human Dignity and Equality

Outrages dishonor those who inflict them far more than those who suffer them. Every time an Arab or an Indochinese is insulted without being able to answer back, beaten without being able to fight back, starved without being able to protest, killed without recourse to justice, it is France that is dishonored. And she is dishonored in this way, alas, every day.

[A 1938 remark of Simone Weil from *Simone Weil On Colonialism*]

I knew as well as I knew anything that the oppressor must be liberated just as surely as the oppressed. A man who takes away another man's freedom is a prisoner of hatred, he is locked behind the bars of prejudice and narrow-mindedness. The oppressed and the oppressor alike are robbed of their humanity.

[Nelson Mandela, *Long Walk to Freedom*]

The historical reversals made possible by the end to colonialism and apartheid, and the prospect of having a voice in a world forum for poorer or smaller nations enhanced by the creation of the United Nations and its Universal Declaration of Human Rights (1948), could be said to be a "victory for justice." But, of course, the benefits of such a victory—freedom, equality, and full citizenship and economic restitution—are elusive and slow in coming, particularly when a global sense of equality "for all" and moral obligation and trust are diminished. The generations of embedded racism and moral and economic inequality are not easily removed. We must look at some of the impediments to the restoration of our humanity, and toward a clearer sense of human respect and equality to move us closer to a meaningful account of what justice should be.

We will first look at the "Mabo case" where aboriginal Australians, dispossessed of their land and livelihood, had their land reinstated by their country's highest court. Several interesting features of how humans treat their neighbors are focused in this example. This is a dramatic precedent for justice in Australia, but also speaks to dispossessed peoples on every continent, especially those freed from colonialism's oppression but who have not yet been able to experience their full equality and humanity.

In the second case we look back through much of the twentieth century when European colonialism was being seriously challenged by both its victims and by those among the colonizers who call our attention to the *injustices* at the very core of colonialism. Our examples in the second case are focused through the lens of a young critic of French colonialism in Southeast Asia and Africa. The young critic was Simone Weil during the period from 1930 to 1943—from about age twenty to her untimely death during World War II—well before *The UN Declaration of Human Rights*. The struggle for justice from European colonial control, from racism in the Americas and southern Africa, and sexism throughout the globe, raged through the twentieth century and lingers in multiple forms in the so-called "post-colonial" present century. It is from such experiences, as we shall see, that insight can be gained into the critical importance of human dignity and equality for understanding the very meaning of justice.

THE IDEA OF JUSTICE BEYOND FAIRNESS

Raimond Gaita writes:

> In 1992 the High Court of Australia granted Australian Aborigines native title to some lands taken from them when the continent was settled. The court's decision was in response to Eddie Mabo's petition for native title in part of the Meriam Islands, off the coast of Queensland. The case is now generally referred to as "Mabo."[1]

In the Mabo case, the Australian justices were unequivocally clear in their judgment that the Australian Aborigines had been unjustly dispossessed of their land, livelihood, and humanity. Justice Brennan wrote:

> According to the cases, the common law itself took from indigenous inhabitants any right to occupy their traditional land, exposed them to deprivation of the religious, cultural and economic sustenance which the land provides, vested the land effectively in the control of the Imperial authority without any right to com-

pensation and made the indigenous inhabitants intruders in their own homes and mendicants for a place to live. Judged by any civilized standard, such a law is unjust and its claim to be part of the common law to be applied in contemporary Australia must be questioned.[2]

Gaita in his extended discussion of "Mabo" in his chapter "Justice Beyond Fairness: Mabo and Social Justice," focuses on the idea that "justice" goes beyond "fairness" and it is this that gives human beings their humanity. Gaita writes: "If I am right to claim that the High Court's judgment on Mabo was the acknowledgment that they [the Aborigines], like the white settlers, had relations to the land that would make dispossession a terrible crime; and if I am also right in claiming that acknowledgment to be an act of justice, then it is justice of a kind that could only be parodied in the claim that the Aborigines had at last been treated decently [or fairly]." "Fairness is at issue," says Gaita, "only when the full human status of those who are protesting their unfair treatment is not disputed."[3]

This example goes to show a central point of Gaita's book that *justice* is not a species of *fairness* but one of equality of respect; that *justice* transcends the law and its practicality; that justice goes *beyond fairness*. He wants to show that the idea of justice *presupposes* full recognition of another's humanity. "Treat me as a human being," he writes, "fully as your equal, without condescension—that demand (or plea), whether it is made by women to men or by blacks to whites, is a demand or a plea for justice. Not, however, for justice conceived as equal access to goods and opportunities. It is for justice conceived as equality of respect."[4]

Short of such equality of respect, there is the specter of racism [or sexism]. Gaita argues that racism or sexism is a form of injustice. He says, "Racism . . . is best characterized as an incapacity on the part of racists to see that anything *could go deep in the inner lives of their victims*."[5] This is similar to the idea discussed in Chapter 1 about "facing" one's neighbor, or refusing to do so. To refuse to "face" one's neighbor, to not acknowledge the other's humanity shows a lack of respect. Such a refusal is to make the other "invisible;" to dis-*regard* them. Or another and more direct way of saying this is found in American black writer, James Baldwin's "Fifth Avenue Uptown." Baldwin writes: "*Negroes want to be treated like men* . . . People who have mastered Kant, Hegel, Shakespeare, Marx, Freud, and *The Bible* find this [perfectly straightforward seven word] statement impenetrable."[6] That is what racism means—to be denied one's humanity. In South Africa, under the *apartheid* regime, the white Afrikaners not only refused to face non-whites, they literally tried to remove them from sight. This was not only a "token" of disrespect, it was a gross act of human denial.

Peter Winch in his book *Simone Weil: "The Just Balance"* says justice is to be considered not just as a moral or "social ideal to be striven for, but as *a point of view* from which alone a certain sort of understanding of human life is possible: as an epistemological concept, therefore."[7] Thus beyond fairness, justice is "facing," "reading," or "going up to" the other. Justice is not caught up in an "equal exchange" or even "fairness" alone, it is an attentive point of view where I begin "to understand *myself* from the standpoint of *the other's* affliction, to understand that my privileged position is not part of my essential nature, but an accident of fate."[8]

There have been many ways in which the idea of one's humanity and the effects of racism have denied such humanity of many peoples: slave trade both ancient and modern (all forms of human trafficking), genocide, forced removals from land or dispossession of land as was common in colonialism, the totalitarian and *apartheid* regimes of the past century, and racial and sexual discrimination. Recently, an article appeared in the Johannesburg *Sunday Independent* newspaper, October 22, 2006. The headline read "Giving Back to Australia's Stolen People." Like the Mabo case, this was about "Australia's treatment of its indigenous people" and how this "remains a running sore." The plight of the "stolen generation" is a principal reason. This was a terrible diminishing of humanity that took place in Australia from 1904 to 1975. One of its goals was to "breed out the Aborigines' color." Now, however, in the state of Tasmania, the state premier, Paul Lennon, unveiled a five-million-dollar reparation plan to compensate surviving members of this generation. The premier said of this initiative: "It's about recognizing that, in Tasmania's history, Aboriginal people were dispossessed of their land, severed from their culture and taken from their families. . . . It's about saying that we're sorry that this happened."[9]

There are also smaller ways of denial of one's humanity—racial jokes or slurs, denial of access to "one's group," simply ignoring one's presence. In what is now called a post-colonial era it is appropriate to examine how colonial powers denied the humanity of those colonized, to remind ourselves not to repeat such a past, and to remind ourselves how we have not effectively given up on the behavior of "colonizing" others.

In the following section, I want to turn the reader's attention again to a remarkable set of insights made by Simone Weil during the 1930s. They reflect her distress as a young woman regarding the behavior of her own country as a "colonial power" during the early decades of the twentieth century. They also unveil to the reader her preoccupation with the meaning of the very idea of justice and injustice. I believe they clearly illustrate Gaita's concern about seeing or not seeing that another human being has "depth." Her insights also speak clearly to the dangers of contemporary forms of oppression in terms of

the global economic dominance of capitalism—a new kind of colonialism—
and the dangers of post-cold-war Imperialism and its backlash from a variety
of kinds of religious fundamentalisms. This last point will be taken up again
in Chapter 6 with respect to issues of colonialism in the twenty-first century.

SEEING THE OTHER WITH EQUAL RESPECT THROUGH THE INJUSTICE OF COLONIALISM

To underscore the importance of equality and mutual respect in thinking
about justice we will explore the very personal reflections of Simone Weil as
collected and translated in the recent book *Simone Weil on Colonialism: An
Ethic of the Other*.[10] A significant number of the selections by Simone Weil
in this book had not been previously published and few had been translated
into English.[11] Also included in this volume are translations of additional
texts by Louis Roubaud, Albert Londres, Félicien Challaye, and Emile Der-
menghen—three French journalists and a celebrated historian, each of whom
had traveled in countries colonized by France and reported on their conditions
in the 1920s and 1930s. Reading these texts in the early 1930s helped Simone
Weil shape her views on suffering, oppression, and justice as compassion.

In writings on Simone Weil, her views of colonialism have been given little notice.[12] However, a strong undercurrent in her own larger writings is that
European civilization should take *inspiration* from "the East." It becomes
very clear in these writings on colonialism that in addition to intense reading
of some of the classical sources of "the East"—Taoist texts, the *Bhagavad-
Gita*, *The Egyptian Book of the Dead*, and a few Buddhist texts—she also
took "inspiration" from reports found in French journals and newspapers during the 1930s and other published accounts like André Gide's *Voyage Au
Congo* and *Retour de Tchad* that focused on European colonial interests. With
respect to the more contemporary sources, she was most interested in the
French colonial links with Indochina and North Africa (especially Algeria)
but was also deeply aware of the situation in French Equatorial Africa. With
respect to Africa, she says that Europeans are largely responsible for the current state of "this unhappy continent," where "the White man . . . had caused
the greatest possible havoc over four centuries."[13]

But what, we might ask, could be taken as "inspiration" from the experience in all these French colonies? Of great importance to Simone Weil was
the sense of rootedness, of loyalty and community found in their traditional
agrarian cultures, and the sense of a spiritual and cultural location with a long
past. She remarked: "They [had] not lost [their] civilizations in a sea of
materialism." She believed that "the chief evil of colonization [was] that it

deprives people of its past," uprooting them from their spiritual location. This was true of all European colonial nations. Judge Brennan of the Australian High Court echoed these sentiments when he wrote the dispossession of the Aborigines land "made the indigenous inhabitants intruders in their own homes and mendicants for a place to live," and that such dispossession was a terrible injustice.

It was also "inspiration" taken from the East and from Africa that contributed to Simone Weil's sensibilities for suffering and affliction, human respect, and justice from the early 1930s to her death. For example, one might easily imagine the young Simone Weil—then about twenty-one years old—collecting vivid images that fed her imagination after reading the following passages from Félicien Challaye's reflections in *Memories of Colonization*. Challaye writes:

> Born of war, colonization partakes of the criminal and montrously stupid character of war itself. The colonial regime is only another form of war.
>
> In primitive societies, it has happened that cannibalism has been a cause of war: the conquerors killed and ate the conquered. One could maintain that the capitalists of the ruling countries eat, in their own way, the proletarians of the subject countries. The concessionaries of the Congolese companies, in the space of thirty years, have consumed around fifteen million blacks.[14]
>
> The colonial regime is not the humanitarian enterprise that its apologists celebrate; it is essentially a *regime of political domination with a view to economic exploitation.*[15]
>
> After war—or rather with war of which it is a consequence and another form—colonization is perhaps the institution that has caused the most pain, has caused the most tears to be shed.
>
> We must put an end to these evils. We must extend to the "colored" people the right to free self determination, we must work towards the liberation of the colonies. (1935)[16]

Keeping in mind her essay *The Iliad* and its focus on force and its counterpoint justice, Simone Weil must have been struck by reading Louis Roubaud's account of the trial of N'Guyan Thai Hoc following the Yen-Bay Massacre in Vietnam by the French. The young N'Guyan was nicknamed the "Great Teacher." The Great Teacher refused to testify but said only "I appear before force and not justice." Roubaud had read an earlier letter written by the young N'Guyan from prison to the French Deputies. Roubaud reports:

> This document, written in bad French, is too long to reproduce in full. I transcribe here a few passages . . . scrupulously respecting the meaning. [Among his few passages is this:]
>   "Deputies:

In justice: the right of every citizen is to wish for freedom for his native land. In humanity: the duty of every individual is to help his brother in misfortune."[17]

One could hardly find a more elegant and compelling expression of mutual recognition for human dignity, freedom, and equality as fundamental to justice.

In her "Introduction," Patricia Little writes: "Simone Weil's writings on colonialism . . . are for the most part hard-hitting, passionate denunciations of the way in which France, the colonial power, wielded power over the powerless inhabitants of her colonial territories, real people with whom, in her boundless capacity to feel the sufferings of the unknown and the dispossessed, she was able to feel in total empathy."[18]

Little also notes that it is known that Simone Weil's family developed a close friendship with an "Annamite" [Vietnamese], N'guyen Van Danh, from whom Simone Weil "must have gleaned a considerable amount of information regarding the situation in Indochina." What really opened her eyes to French colonialism was the reporting by Louis Roubaud in *Le Petit Parisien* of the massacre of Yen-Bay in Indochina in 1930. Little says, "she makes it quite clear that reading Roubaud's articles [plus reading about the 'Colonial Exhibition of 1931' in Paris] had opened her eyes once and for all to the horrors of the colonial system."[19] Simone Weil said that reading these accounts evoked a sense of shame in her beloved France for the first time.

The "1931 Colonial Exhibition" had painted a picture of "*la Plus Grande France.*" She immediately saw, notes Little, "the scandalous contrast between image and reality." There were protests at the Exhibition by Surrealists André Breton, Paul Eluard, and others in a show of solidarity between French workers and those in the colonies. This all took place at the time of the publication of André Gide's *Voyage Au Congo* and *Retour de Tchad* "in which [Gide] denounces the terrible mortality among the wretched natives hounded down like beasts to work in appalling conditions on the [construction of the Congo-Océan railway in the French Congo]."[20] The scandal had been documented by Albert Londres and others. In spite of this convergence and the new awareness of artists and some politicians, there were few voices raised against the colonial system.

Curiously, this was also the time when a young Leopold Senghor, Aimé Césaire, and other black intellectuals were meeting around the University of Paris and giving shape to what became the Negritude Movement in Africa. There is no evidence I am aware of that suggests Simone Weil was conscious of that development unfolding in her backyard—a development that was very much linked to the colonial scandals. Senghor's circle took place during a critical period when Simone Weil was *not* based in Paris. Much of the potential for a serious anti-colonial movement in France would defer to the buildup leading to World War II. Even the Negritude Movement that helped spark liberation movements in west and central African nations would be put on hold until after the war. It was, however, during this period of the 1930s that Simone Weil's views on French colonialism were formed, and they developed around the moral considerations of dignity for all human beings and the alleviation of human suffering. She believed that the colonial system was inherently unjust—"it was an illegitimate ownership of human flesh."[21] Let us now turn in more detail to the larger range of themes that Simone Weil developed in this period that correspond with her writing on colonialism.

Little writes: "Simone Weil's criticism of the colonial system is based broadly speaking on two grounds: the physical and moral abuses committed against the subject populations, and the way in which they have been uprooted from their native culture."[22] A further point mentioned above is that colonialism "deprives a person of his or her freedom or capacity to consent." This latter idea receives increasing attention in the latter part of Simone Weil's writings. In her essay "Are We Struggling for Justice?" written in London, Weil writes:

> Where obedience is consented to there is freedom: there and nowhere else.
> Where there is agreement by mutual consent there is justice. . . .
> Consent is neither to be bought nor sold, . . . in a society where monetary transactions dominate most of social life, where almost all obedience is bought and sold, there can be no freedom.
> Where people know no motives other than constraint, money, and a carefully maintained and stimulated enthusiasm, there is no possibility of freedom.
> That on the whole is the case today, in varying degrees in all the countries of the white race, and in all those where the influence of the white race has penetrated.[23]

After the war the struggle for justice *is* picked up by liberation movements in North Africa, French Equatorial Africa, and Indochina. These were struggles that lifted up the past and traditions of those who had lost their capacity to consent and who knew only a life of constraint by the white race!

There can be little doubt that the peoples dominated by the French had known physical hardship throughout their histories. This was not so much the issue as was the fact that the colonizers had turned physical hardship into a tool of domination that destroyed the human spirit and denied the dignity of those dominated. Physical hardship was turned into spiritual and cultural death.

Simone Weil argued that the way out of the colonial quagmire was to turn subjects into citizens and allow them to participate in their own lawmaking.

Of course what happened in many colonies, especially the British and French colonies, was to install what was called "customary law" or "the Native Code"—a parallel law whereby "tribal communities" could partially govern their own affairs. Not only did this lead to the segregating of cultures, it also gave the colonial governing powers a veto over any customary practices. This was, in fact, *rule by coercion and not consent.*[24]

It is in *The Need for Roots* and *London Writings* that Simone Weil's boldest thoughts on colonialism are expressed. Here, one focus is on the obligations that one should have toward human beings. The central obligation is mutual respect as we have been arguing, and this applies at all times and in all places to "earthly needs" as well as "spiritual needs." This she holds as "sacred." I again note, as Little also has, that her appeal is not to the secular "rights" of human beings that imply promoting a form of individual rights—rather, she appeals to an idea of justice that transcends what is now understood as justice based on individual rights. Justice is simply, Simone Weil writes, echoing Socrates, "seeing that no harm is done to men" (period).[25] This is why, as Little notes, "The abuses [Simone Weil] read about in Louis Roubaud's account of the situation in Indochina, and found in Albert Londres and Félicien Challaye, are radically unacceptable."[26]

Following are a few quotations from Simone Weil's texts on colonialism, accompanied by comments of my own. With a little of the reader's imagination exercised, the contemporary relevance of these quotations for rethinking the idea of justice should be very clear.

[From 1933–1934]: It's the same problem as that of capitalism. You colonize to develop commerce, not for the well being of the colonized.

We can *resumé* the question of colonization by the following table:

Benefits: roads, railways, factories, hospitals, schools, destruction of superstitions and family oppression (the yoke which burdens women, etc.).

Disadvantages or horrors: See the articles in *Le Petit Parisien* published by Louis Roubaud. Corporal punishments, massacres, bombings; the French masses do not care about the fact that an overseer can massacre a native with impunity. . . . See Gide: Congo, forced labor; it has been calculated that every meter of railway cost one human life.[27]

[From 1936–1937]: It is with feelings of pain and shame that I, a young Frenchwoman who has never left Europe, am writing to the Indochinese through the intermediary of this newspaper. This pain and shame go back a long way. More than five years. For more than five years they have constantly weighed me down. . . . Since that time, I have never been able to think of Indochina without feeling ashamed of my country.[28]

[In response to the above claims she later writes]: When I think of a future possible war, the feelings of fear and horror which such an image evokes in me are mingled with a slightly reassuring thought, that a European war could well perhaps signal the revenge of the colonial peoples to punish our lack of concern, our indifference and our cruelty.

It is not a joyful prospect, but the need for imminent justice finds in it a certain satisfaction.[29]

This is, truly, a hard set of remarks coming from Simone Weil. It is also counterintuitive to her "sense" of justice—to "signal revenge" of the colonized people to punish France for its cruelty and to take some satisfaction in that! Clearly what is seen by her is the total disregard—the lack of any form of "attention" to those colonized. Or, as Gaita argues, there is no recognition of depth in the other, and thus no guilt or shame in the acts of dispossession or harm to them.

Simone Weil's cynicism in her earliest responses to French colonial control in Morocco, and its posturing with the English and Germans before World War I broke out, sound familiar to us today. She playfully chides that France acted as if "the territory of the fatherland was threatened."

[From 1937]: Yes, the territory of the fatherland was threatened. Which part of the territory, in fact? Alsace-Lorraine? Yes, precisely that. Or rather no, not exactly Alsace-Lorraine, but something equivalent. It was Morocco. Yes, Morocco, that quintessentially French province. . . . Morocco has always been a part of France. Or if not always, at least from time immemorial (well, almost). Yes, precisely since December 1911.

Indeed, that's what appears even more clearly if one looks at the history of Morocco. That history must make even the most indifferent feel that Morocco is in some ways a second Lorraine for France.[30]

Indeed, the American and the British might be heard in conversation to say Iraq threatened the fatherland; it is like (at least almost) a second northern slope of Alaska or the Falklands; it has always been ours and we must protect it by invading it!

Consider the following passages concerning France's treatment of North Africans with the current parallel in South Africa that the apartheid regime is more to be *dishonored* than those who suffered from their outrages. Or, is there a parallel to be drawn with an American pre-emption for Empire?

[From 1938]: Outrages dishonor those who inflict them far more than those who suffer them. Every time an Arab or an Indochinese is insulted without being able to answer back, beaten without being able to fight back, starved without being able to protest, killed without recourse to justice, it is France that is dishonored. And she is dishonored in this way, alas, every day.

But the most bloody outrage occurs when she constrains those whom she deprives of their dignity, their freedom and their fatherland, to go and die for the dignity, the freedom and the fatherland of their masters. In antiquity, there were slaves, but it was only the citizens who fought wars. Today we have invented something better; we first of all reduce whole populations to slavery, and then we use them as cannon-fodder.[31]

The following passages concern French attitudes toward the death of Arabs and Annamites [Vietnamese]:

[From 1938]: Those people are too far away, it's said. No! They are not far away. Peoples under France's domination, whose wretchedness or well-being, shame or dignity, and sometimes their very lives, depend entirely on French policies, are as close to us as the very places where those policies are devised.

Besides, these territories are coming closer to us; they will come even closer in the future. They will come closer, in terms of the French imagination, in so far as French people feel that they threaten the security of France. . . . I am among those who think that all problems regarding the colonies should be posed above all in terms of their relationships with the aspirations, the freedoms and the well-being of the colonized peoples, and only secondarily in terms of their relationship with the interests of the colonizing nation.[32]

There is a sense in which all nations of the world have come closer to one another—a truism that we in America seem to ignore in denouncing treaties, bypassing the U.N., selectively choosing if and when to participate in international law and its courts, and pursuing only what clearly is in our economic and political interest. We must come to see that their—the other's—problems have become increasingly our problems; that our well-being is connected to their well-being. For example, we Americans have failed to respect the well-being of ordinary Iraqi citizens, and in doing so have undermined all respect, trust, or goodwill that we may have once commanded around the globe. Where is there justice in this behavior?

Here are three passages from one of Simone Weil's longer essays from 1938 that outline some positive ways that a partnership between France and its colonies could be forged.

The colonizing nations [should have] an interest in the progressive emancipation of her colonies, and that she is conscious of that interest. Now the conditions of such a solution exists. The play of international forces is such that France has an interest, an urgent and obvious interest in transforming her subjects into partners. She must understand that interest; and it is here that propaganda can play a part.

It is indispensable that French subjects have something of their own which they would be likely to love under another rule; and to that effect it is indispensable that they cease being subjects, in other words passive beings, well or badly treated, but completely subject to the treatment meted out to them. They must start the process, soon and quite rapidly, of evolution from status of subject to that of citizen.

The past, the traditions, the beliefs of each people must be taken into account. But whatever the structure decided upon, success is only possible if it is inspired by the same urgent necessity: the populations of the colonies must participate actively in their own interest in the political and economic life of their country.[33]

Finally, perhaps her most important and comprehensive essay was written in London in 1943, titled: "Concerning the Colonial Question in its Relationship with the Destiny of the French People." It was not published in her lifetime. Here she stresses the "inspiration" that can be drawn from "the East," which by now would include what she had come to appreciate from the French colonial experience in Africa and Indochina as well as the classical texts she loved. In this essay it is the people, their humanity, and aspects of their past that is the focus of her attention. I will conclude with just a few summary reflections drawn from this essay. You will see how this essay embraces many of the components of her concerns that we have touched upon, and on our larger concern for respect and dignity of all human beings as a necessary condition for justice.

Two focal points for her remarks are that: (1) a colonial power or one country never has "the right to determine the destiny [of another people]," and (2) when another country is deprived of its past by being uprooted by force, "the loss of the past is the descent into colonial enslavement." Such a denial or loss, "make these populations literally die of sadness, by forbidding their customs, their traditions, their celebrations, their whole enjoyment of life."[34] [This is a theme that will later pervade the pages of Frantz Fanon.]

Simone Weil discussed three temptations that any nation should overcome: "*The first temptation* is a sort of patriotism which tends to prefer its own country to justice."[35] Not to deny an appropriate patriotism, but she believed that the concerns of justice should override those of patriotism or nationalism. "I am French," she says. "But I believe in seeking for justice and truth before power and prosperity for one's self, one's family and one's country." This is a terrible temptation taken up all too often by Americans—a false patriotism that fails to seek justice and truth before power and prosperity.

The second temptation is to "turn to the experts. The experts, in this matter are the colonials." Too often there is the temptation to ignore the past of any country you colonize; to not respect its language and culture. She says of French colonials that they "are not generally curious about the history of the countries where they are based." She concludes that we should not trust the "colonials, that is, the Governor and bureaucrats in the colonies."[36]

The third temptation is particularly relevant to present day global concerns; it is what she calls "The Christian temptation." This is the temptation to see colonialism as creating "a favorable environment for missions." Christians, she says, tend to love colonialism for that reason. Furthermore, Christian missionaries seldom, if ever, raise the question "as to whether a Hindu, a Buddhist, a Muslim or one of those termed pagan has not in his own tradition a path towards that spirituality which the Christian churches offer him." In any case, she concludes, "Christ never said that warships should accompany, even at a distance, those who bring the good news. Their presence changes the nature of the message. You are asking for more trumps in your hand than are allowed when you want at one and the same time Caesar and the Cross."[37]

I would identify a "fourth" temptation—though one she does not label a temptation—that of transforming what is said to be an expedition related to security policy into conquest. She writes: "as often happens [and happened in Algeria], defense is transformed into conquest." May we in the United States, today, be spared such a consequence in the name of "security policy." We must avoid a new era of imperialism, especially as our world is becoming an interlocking whole of diverse peoples, cultures, and religious beliefs. Should the United States fail in this temptation, then the vengeance of the world will turn upon us.[38]

It should be said that the United States government has already failed in this temptation. In our venture in Iraq, our failure to show much compassion for Darfur, our bullying of nations who fail to do as our government demands, we can already see that vengeance has been unleashed in response to our arrogance. We have managed to turn our retribution for terrorist attacks into a greater menace of terror—the hatred of a large portion of the Muslim world. Where is the justice in this?

I will close with this prescient insight of Simone Weil that follows from the "fourth" temptation. One of her greatest fears from the mid-1930s to her death in 1943 was what she called "the Americanization of Europe"—even, she said, the "Americanization of the terrestrial globe." She believed that American culture would rob Europe of the little, but precious, "inspiration" it had gained from "the East." Europe, she said, needed periodically "real contact with the East in order to remain spiritually alive." It is not just Europe that periodically needs contact with and respect for the larger world—especially Africa and the East—to keep it "spiritually alive!" This unusual sense of global human respect and cultural balance should be lifted up in all of our social, political, and religious education and embedded into our diplomacy and daily affairs if the outcome of our policies toward others is to be just. Perhaps even short of "just" we could settle for enough mutual respect between the cultures driven by the three Abrahamic religions, Judaism, Christianity, and Islam, to sustain some peace and civility. The very thought of the "Americanization" or the dominance of Islam or any religious fundamentalism or the ideological totalization of cultures (as was the goal of Hitler's German Reichstag and former Soviet socialism) is incompatible with the very idea of justice. It is not just "incompatible"—it is an act of aggression—an act of arrogant disrespect, an act that denies the dignity of the "other." How can a sense of global justice prosper in a climate of unwarranted aggression?

NOTES

1. Raimond Gaita, *A Common Humanity: Thinking about Love and Truth and Justice* (London: Routledge, 2000), 73.

2. Gaita, *A Common Humanity*, 77.

3. Gaita, *A Common Humanity*, 9, 81.

4. Gaita, *A Common Humanity*, xx.

5. Gaita, *A Common Humanity*, xxv. My emphasis.

6. James Baldwin, "Fifth Avenue, Uptown," *Esquire*, June 1960. Reprinted in Baldwin, *The Price of the Ticket* (New York: St. Martins, 1985), 211. My emphasis.

For more philosophical discussions of racism see K. A. Appiah, *In My Father's House: Africa in the Philosophy of Culture* (New York: Oxford University Press, 1992), especially Chapter Two; and Franz Fanon, *Toward the African Revolution* (Monthly Review Press, 1988).

7. Peter Winch, *Simone Weil: "The Just Balance"* (Cambridge: Cambridge University Press, 1989), 179.

8. Winch, *Simone Weil*, 182.

9. Sunday Independent (Johannesburg, October 22, 2006). Reported by Kathy Marks.

10. J. P. Little, *Simone Weil on Colonialism: An Ethic of the Other*, trans., edited and introduced by J. P. Little (Lanham, MD: Rowman & Littlefield, 2003).

11. Two of the pieces, "About the Problems of the French Empire" and "Treatment of Negro War-prisoners from the French Army," were written in English by Simone Weil during her short stay in New York City between July and November, 1942. These were previously presented by J. P. Little under the overall title "Textes inédits de New York," with a French translation by Georges Charot, in *Cahiers Simone Weil*, 22, 3 (September 1999): 229–56.

12. My remarks reflect my own selected use of the texts to focus on a few issues that bring Simone Weil's thoughts closer to some of our own present day moral concerns about cross-cultural justice, empire, and human suffering.

13. Little, *Simone Weil on Colonialism*, 109.

14. Little, *Simone Weil on Colonialism*, 195.

15. Little, *Simone Weil on Colonialism*, 196.

16. Little, *Simone Weil on Colonialism*, 199.

17. Little, *Simone Weil on Colonialism,* 142.

18. Little, *Simone Weil on Colonialism,* 1.

19. Little, *Simone Weil on Colonialism,* 7.

20. Little, *Simone Weil on Colonialism,* 9.

21. Little, *Simone Weil on Colonialism,* 14, 124.

22. Little, *Simone Weil on Colonialism,* 14.

23. Simone Weil, "Are We Struggling for Justice?" *Philosophical Investigations* 10:1 (January 1987): 1, 6, 7.

24. An excellent discussion of the negative effects of British colonialism and its "customary law" can be found in Mahmood Mamdani, *Citizen and Subject: Contemporary Africa and The Legacy of Late Colonialism* (Princeton: Princeton University Press 1996), especially Part I.

25. See my *Simone Weil: The Way of Justice as Compassion,* chapters 3, 4, and 5.

26. Little, *Simone Weil on Colonialism,* 22.

27. Little, *Simone Weil on Colonialism,* 27f.

28. Little, *Simone Weil on Colonialism,* 29f.

29. Little, *Simone Weil on Colonialism,* 44.

30. Little, *Simone Weil on Colonialism,* 31f.

31. Little, *Simone Weil on Colonialism,* 48f.

32. Little, *Simone Weil on Colonialism,* 64.

33. Little, *Simone Weil on Colonialism,* 68–70.

34. Little, *Simone Weil on Colonialism,* 110.

35. Little, *Simone Weil on Colonialism,* 107.

36. Little, *Simone Weil on Colonialism,* 107f.

37. Little, *Simone Weil on Colonialism,* 108.

38. Such vengeance has already been unleashed in our venture in Iraq. Its full consequences are yet to be understood.

Chapter Three

Justice: Mercy and the Cultivation of Humanity

It is only through the widest possible compilation of people's perceptions, stories, myths and experiences . . . [that we] can restore memory and foster a new humanity . . . [and that this is] perhaps justice in its deepest sense.

[Antjie Krog, *Country of My Skull*]

In this chapter we will pick up some threads from Chapter 1 where the views of justice in Greek and Roman antiquity were introduced. Of particular interest is what Martha Nussbaum identified as "the equity tradition" and the importance of mercy and forgiveness in rethinking justice. We will also move closer to what Seneca called the "cultivation of humanity," then broach the question of forgiveness and reconciliation in cross-cultural justice by looking at the example of the South African Commission on Truth and Reconciliation (TRC). In its quest for equity through its process of victims' hearings and amnesty procedures after the fall of apartheid, the TRC cleared the way to "foster a new humanity" and promote justice in the new South Africa.

MERCY AND "THE EQUITY TRADITION"

Andrew Brien in his essay "Mercy Within Legal Justice," like Nussbaum, takes the ideas of the ancient Greeks and later Seneca to help us understand justice as moving the policies and actions of individuals, communities, and governments toward, what he calls, "moral outcomes." He believes that if one wants a legal justice system that is not simply concerned with "what one is owed," or that seeks some static end, but desires a justice system that "aims for moral outcomes," then mercy and equity are required in legal justice. This insight goes beyond local vision and casts our gaze on the situation of each human being judged—both local citizens of a community or a stranger in their midst. He believes that mercy is a virtue that can be cultivated by each individual as well as a disposition taken by a court or a judge. In fact, if it is part of one's legal system it is likely to dispose the citizens of that system in the direction of a merciful attitude toward others as well. Brien goes on to say:

> Mercy provides sight to the moral agent; it enables her to perceive, be sensitive to, and understand the world, and to evaluate the salient moral properties of the people with whom she has contact. This virtue enables an actor to use power wisely. Without mercy, those dark passions that blind the framers and implementers of public policy to important facts about people, and lead them to focus instead only upon desert, are even more unchecked. Therefore, in order that institutional actors not exercise their discretionary powers in an undirected and morally blind manner but in a wise and proper way, informed by moral considerations and in ways that promote public well-being, society ought to encourage actors to cultivate a merciful stance.[1]

What Brien calls "this gentle virtue" of mercy, "promotes a humanizing and civilizing effect in a world in which the inhabitants are almost continually surrounded by violence and gratuitous displays of power and domination." This virtue, he says, "brings into the world those sorts of actions that break the cycle of revenge and retribution . . . [and] it promotes harmony in the community, reconciliation and flourishing."[2]

Aristotle is attributed with integrating "equity" into the concept of justice. This clearly reinstates the moral agent into the role of interpreting and carrying out the written law. Aristotle, says Nussbaum, tells "us that the equitable person is characterized by a forgiving attitude to 'human things.'" This attitude requires that one must "judge with" the agent who has done the alleged wrong, or learn to sympathize and see the issues from the point of view of the other or the offender.[3] The idea of "judging with" and "learning to sympathize" would also encourage a legal system that would promote "moral outcomes." This, of course, is one of Aristotle's aims for the moral agent. We will further discuss Nussbaum's interpretation of Aristotle's notion of "judging with" in our next chapter when we turn to the concept of "sympathetic understanding" as a tool for rethinking justice across boundaries.

Nussbaum carries forward some of Aristotle's ideas as she sees them taking a more concrete shape in the idea of mercy in Seneca's writings. She notes that "Seneca begins his argument in *On Anger* as an Aristotelian would, asking the judge to look at all the circumstances of the offense," or, as we noted earlier, "to get the whole story." She interprets Seneca as developing "a merciful attitude . . . regarding each particular case as a complex narrative of human effort in a world of obstacles." She continues:

> The merciful judge will not fail to judge the guilt of the offender, but she will also see the many obstacles this offender faced on the way to being just—as a member of a culture, a gender, a city or country, and, above all, as a member of the human species, facing the obstacles characteristic of human life in a world of scarcity and accident.[4]

"Seneca's bet," says Nussbaum, "is that once one performs this imaginative exercise one will cease to have the strict retributive attitude to the punishment of the offender."[5] This is a bet that few legal theorists and political philosophers (not to mention politicians) have been willing to take in recent decades—perhaps due to the skeptical frame of mind imbued by our Western retributive culture.

It is often thought that mercy "merely" tempers justice on some occasions. To think this keeps the two concepts separate—as if when "justice" (retributive response) gets too overbearing then add a little "mercy." Aristotle, Seneca, Brien, and Nussbaum understand mercy with respect to justice differently. To them *mercy is a part of the meaning of justice*, and where it is not seen as part of "being just," then you have lost something of the very meaning of justice. Jonathan Sacks notes that one of Judaism's sages said: "In the beginning, God sought to create the world through the attribute of justice but He saw that it could not stand. What then did He do? He took justice and joined it to the attribute of mercy."[6] The justice *joined* with mercy creates a new concept of justice that infuses it with forgiveness and with compassion; it changes the sense of justice from a 1:1 (deserts, retributive concept of justice) to one that has built into it a "forgiving or merciful attitude"—a sense of justice that always embraces the possibility of forgiveness and reconciliation, of "restoring" a balance that through retribution may, at anytime, spin out of control. Justice as retribution "will not stand"; it must be "joined with mercy."

Little seems to have changed from Seneca's time to ours. There is no less scarcity of need, no fewer obstacles, nor what we call "accidents" of life. Now, however, some "accidents" of life have compounded by intention to premeditated terror and the weapons of terror have proportionally outstripped our conception of "accidents." Thus the "narrative of human effort" and people's stories have become more complex. The human spirit must find more imaginative resources to navigate the world. Regarding justice, it seems simpler today to respond to offenders with a "retributive attitude" rather than a "merciful or forgiving attitude"—the symmetry seems "neater." The more obstacles there are, however, the greater is the *asymmetry* in cases that are to be judged. Thus there is a need for a heightened moral imagination to navigate through the obstacles and to give the proper attention to the offenders' particulars.

Once again a parallel can be seen in the twentieth-century writings of Simone Weil. Although she does not speak specifically of "mercy," the "merciful attitude" is found in her idea of compassion in justice. This comes out in her high view of the role of judges in society. Let us look briefly at her view of how judges might be educated so they can judge with "a merciful or forgiving attitude." She says they must be

> Drawn from very different social circles; be naturally gifted with wide, clear, and exact intelligence; and be trained in a school where they receive *not just a legal education but above all a spiritual one*; and only secondarily an intellectual one. They must be accustomed to love truth.[7]

This "spiritual education" is for the purpose of both recognizing and understanding human obligation and for discerning when peoples' circumstances may have created unmanageable obstacles. A "spiritual education" also serves to enhance the judges' capacity for "attention." The law school must help its students/judges "learn to distinguish between the two cries: Why am I being hurt? and Why has somebody else got more than I have? Then, as gently as possible, to hush the second one with the help of a code of justice, tribunals, and police."[8] Understanding the first cry requires a sense of justice that embraces both equity and mercy or compassion. Simone Weil continually reminds us how the circumstances of life affect our actions. She says: "Justice. To be ever ready to admit that another person is something quite different from what we read when he is there (or when we think about him). Or rather, to read in him that he is certainly something different, perhaps something completely different, from what we read in him. Every being cries out silently to be read differently."[9]

Ron Collins and Finn Nielsen—a legal scholar and political theorist, respectively—in their comprehensive essay "The Spirit of Simone Weil's Law," provide us with the most comprehensive reconstruction of what Simone Weil believed to be the role of equity and mercy/compassion in the practice of the law. They make the following summary remarks that I will quote at some length:

> The notion of equity is most compatible with Weil's view of law. . . . Equity, for Weil, is contextual (the realities of this world) and normative (i.e., the reality outside of this world). Practically speaking, her equitable "system" of law is essentially ex post facto oriented. That is, where laws are not particularized, where they are not concise, they take on meaning only *after* the fact, after a judge has

breathed life into them. Looking at the legal system from the "front end," such rule by equity cannot put the citizenry on actual notice of exactly what conduct is, or is not, prohibited. Yet, for centuries ex post facto laws, at least in the case of penal matters, have been deemed synonymous with tyranny. How would Weil respond to such a charge?

Weil might have answered somewhat along these lines:

Law should not be either in formulation or application static. The more that it tends in that direction, the more it will defeat the high purpose of justice. Citizens, government officials, and judges are not unaware of the law; that is, they are abundantly cognizant of its declaration of principles. Living *in* the laws means living *out* these principles, always attentively applying them to a myriad of situations. Always thinking; always reading. In living out the law, what is most important is the process of continually orienting oneself towards the good. Written laws, seen as "guides," point citizen and judge alike in this direction. In this sense, then, law may take on a concrete meaning after the fact, though it is imbued with meaning from the beginning. Conversely, when the legal realm of right and wrong is neatly packaged in black letter in a code or case, law (seen as a dialectical process) is sapped of its meaning. Weil [believed] the purpose of punishment is therapeutic. It is an inclusive concept (bringing people in), not an exclusive one (sending them out). Punishment removes "the stigma of . . . crime."[10] Punishment, she tells us, can reveal one's mistake, much as a teacher does when helping a pupil to understand an error in geometry. Finally, punishment is redemptive.

Not surprisingly, Weil found it salutary to introduce her concept of punishment into an idea of law for at least two reasons: first, to make possible the dialectical process in the law; and second, to infuse law with an overtly moral purpose. . . .Weil's notion of punishment reintroduced moral questions into politics and thereby *rejects* the idea that there are no truths in this realm. Punishment compels us, and especially our leaders, to face up to the moral matter. If there are no political truths, then there can be no punishment.[11]

It is interesting how Weil views punishment as "therapeutic" and "redemptive." This anticipates contemporary discussions of the limited effects of purely retributive punishment and the prospect that a legal system can be rehabilitative for perpetrators of crime and can "reintroduce moral questions" into politics and justice. We will later look closely at those who promote the dialectical role of "restorative justice" to a legal system to move it toward greater "moral outcomes."

To place the ideas of "the equity tradition" into a practical setting—one that was itself not static but "always thinking, always reading" —let us look at how the recent South African Commission on Truth and Reconciliation [TRC] process embraced these ideas. Here we will discover clearly that a meaningful concept of justice should, as Brien said, "aim for moral outcomes" or as

Collins and Nielsen, interpreting Simone Weil say, the law must be "infused with an overtly moral purpose." In considering punishment for perpetrators of political crimes, *the TRC had to be attentive to the truth in the context of evil and political struggle*. Part of the very idea of this commission was to "orient oneself toward the good" and turn the discernment of truth to some "redemptive" purpose; an extremely high purpose, indeed. A purpose, however, that had surprisingly good results in an extremely hostile and volatile political climate.

MERCY AND FORGIVENESS IN PRACTICE: THE SOUTH AFRICAN CASE

Pumla Gobodo-Mandikizela, a clinical psychologist on the TRC, clarifies the parameters within which the Commission worked when she wrote:

> What happened at the Truth commission may not be generalizable to all other situations. But what the work of the TRC suggests is that cycles of political violence can indeed be broken and that there are alternatives to revenge and retributive justice. . . .
>
> An important condition for the possibility of democratization after totalitarian rule is the forging of a vocabulary of compromise and tolerance, especially in the aftermath of mass tragedy.[12]

What does such vocabulary of compromise and tolerance look like?

An important universal moral question in philosophy is, "How does one get to the truth of and deal with human harmdoing and injustice?" In South Africa this question has the particular form: "How does one get to the truth of and deal with the aftermath of apartheid's evil?" This question was confronted directly by the people of South Africa when the new majority government proposed a commission on truth and reconciliation in June 1994 as one of its first orders of business.[13] To get to the truth of apartheid's evil and restore dignity to apartheid's victims were goals of the South African TRC. The process of this Commission over a period of about five years ignited a lively discussion on the possibility of national reconciliation after apartheid, and it challenged the very meaning of the concept of justice for a society in transition. The Commission's chief tool in achieving this end turned out to be the power of the language of its ordinary (and extraordinary) people—the language of truth-telling.

From 1996 to 2000 public testimony of the victims of violence and the perpetrators of violence (victims' hearings and amnesty hearings) painfully unfolded the truth. In the South African situation this truth-telling lifted up the ironies in harmdoing and pointed to the disjunctures in language and life it-self. In the testimonies the logics of denial and mourning somehow coexisted in ways that reveal the truth. We could characterize this process as an imagi-native narrative—a living moral tale.[14] In the best of worlds the TRC process can be understood as a historic dialogue, shaping a new public discourse upon which South Africa might build a new civil society. Of course the Commis-sion did not take place "in the best of worlds," and much of the desired ef-fects have not been immediately realized. Time pressures and politics made for a "less than perfect" process. I will say more on this shortly.

During seven months of the year 2000 (January through July) I was asso-ciated with the philosophy faculty of the University of Stellenbosch outside of Cape Town. Although I sometimes felt like an alien in a strange land, I re-ceived a warm welcome from several faculty members, especially Willie van der Merwe, Wilhelm Verwoerd, and Annie Gagiano. Wilhelm had recently re-turned to teaching having spent two years (1996–1998) as a researcher for the TRC. He also helped write the Commission Report. Annie Gagiano of the English literature faculty could always be counted on to put things into per-spective to allow me to understand the social and political environment of the Afrikaans culture of the university. The Commission's final report had been out for about a year, but the amnesty hearings were still ongoing and com-mentary on the meaning and value of the Commission's work over the past four years and the continuing hearings were being widely debated. It seemed transparent to me, but not to all in this community, how important the debates were for contemporary ethics and political philosophy on a global scale. I be-lieved there was much to be learned from this extraordinary social experiment for understanding the nature of justice as we entered the new millennium.

Following a brief exploratory paper (from an outsider's point of view) on "Justice and the TRC" that I presented to a philosophy research seminar, I was barraged by many skeptical questions. The most difficult of the questions was: "How does 'justice' follow from the Commission's mandate for truth and reconciliation?" The idea of justice simply had no logical connection to these two concepts it was argued. One might uncover some of the truths of the social and political dealings of the past forty years, but not see justice in such revelations. And, if some few persons found some forgiveness and rec-onciliation in their revelations that is well and good, but such revelations still did not add up to justice.[15] It is here that the very concept of justice seems problematic. This was a challenging response and I want to address this chal-lenge. I will answer my interlocutor's question in a deliberately indirect, but I believe, precise manner.

I often ask myself about the value of the frequent calls for victims *to for-give* those who perpetrated terrible acts of injustice that devastated their lives.

Just what is the value of forgiveness when such awful things had broken so many lives? What bearing does forgiveness have on the relation of truth to reconciliation? Nobel Prize laureate Wole Soyinka of Nigeria has given us insight into this question in his book *The Burden of Memory, The Muse of Forgiveness* where he links the "muse of forgiveness" and "the "muse of reconciliation" to Leopold Senghor's attitude toward the French after the independence of Senegal.[16] Soyinka traces with some astonishment how Africans seem to be able to forgive and reconcile enmity after so much suffering and injustice.[17] Thirteen years earlier, in his Nobel lecture (1986), Soyinka had noted that "[t]here is a deep lesson for the world in the black races' capacity to forgive, one which, I often think, has much to do with ethical precepts which spring from their world view and authentic religions, none of which is ever totally eradicated by the accretions of foreign faiths and their implicit ethnocentrism."[18]

Given that this "miracle" of South Africa did happen, what seems almost beyond the miraculous is the fact that leaders like Mandela and his African National Congress did not seek retribution against whites during negotiations with the National Party and the writing of the Interim Constitution. Rather, they sought as had others like Senghor, and continue to seek, *reconciliation* among all South Africans: black and white. This idea, in fact, is deliberately inscribed into the Interim Constitution: "There is a need for understanding but not for vengeance, a need for reparations but not for retaliation, a need for *ubuntu* but not for victimization."[19] This pattern is perhaps most surprising because it is spoken of as a "natural" moral way of being while to Western ears this may seem so "unnatural." How is this possible? What are these "ethical precepts," in Soyinka's words, which "spring from [the African's] world view and authentic religions?" And I add what is embedded in this use of the concept of *ubuntu.*

I will pick up a thread here from the Ghanaian philosopher Kwame Gyekye to try and answer Soyinka's question. Gyekye refers to what he calls "supererogatory acts" where caring, compassion, and generosity are fundamental moral categories intrinsic to a communitarian ethic in Africa that lead persons to give greater attention to other persons and less attention to one's self. This is part of the ethic of *ubuntu.* I believe Gyekye's larger discussion of "communitarianism" has bearing on our understanding of the relation of forgiveness, reconciliation, and justice in some African contexts. Gyekye engages several Western philosophers who reject the value of supererogatory acts in moral theory. John Rawls, for example, believes that although such acts may be good, they are neither intrinsic nor part of one's obligation in being moral, largely because they involve incalculable risks. Those like Rawls who deny the intrinsic qualities of supererogatory acts believe, says Gyekeye, that moral conduct is essentially to be confined to acts that human beings can or want conveniently to perform and that will promote their own individual ends . . . they think that *some* form of self-sacrifice cannot be required of any and every moral agent. But the question is: which form of self-sacrifice can or should be required of the moral agent, and how do we determine that?[20]

Gyekye, on the other hand, believes "generosity" and other supererogatory acts *should be* required of the moral agent. He says:

The scope of our moral responsibilities should not be circumscribed. The moral life, which essentially involves paying regard to the needs, interests, and well-being of *others*, already implies self-sacrifice and loss, that is, loss of something—one's time, money, strength, and so on. There is, in my view, no need, therefore, to place limits on the form of the self-sacrifice and, hence, the extent of our moral responsibilities.[21]

Such generosity promotes the welfare of others, and for Gyekye, it "should be considered a basic moral responsibility," and is so considered in many African societies.

I think there should be little doubt that part of the success of South Africa is the consistency with which the non-white and white ANC leaders—Mandela, Tutu, Mbeki, Ruth First, Albie Sachs, Kader Asmal, even Joe Slovo (the leader of the South African Communist Party)[22]—believed that morality required supererogatory acts. A peaceful transition to majority democracy required a way of acting that implied both self-sacrifice and regard for the well-being of others. There must be inclusion without retribution, and equality for *all* people in spite of the sins of apartheid in the *new* South Africa. Mandela wrote from prison:

I knew as well as I knew anything that the oppressor must be liberated just as surely as the oppressed. A man who takes away another man's freedom is a prisoner of hatred, he is locked behind the bars of prejudice and narrow mindedness . . . . the oppressed and the oppressor alike are robbed of their humanity.[23]

Thinkers like Gyekye, Mandela, Soyinka, and Tutu believe that such acts are natural extensions of a way of life that is characteristic of, if not intrinsic to, an African identity. Acting for the benefit of all relates in part to the development of moral character tied to communitarian-based thinking. In Tutu's case it is also tied to his Christian theological convictions. For Mandela the idea, having been planted in his Xhosa-Thembu upbringing, came to full flower ironically and paradoxically as a consequence of long years of reflection while imprisoned on Robben Island, as well as through his daily encounters, like so many others, with the affliction of his people. The notion of another's needs was always part of Mandela's thinking; he always looked beyond his own self-interest toward his fellow South Africans.[24]

This point is often illustrated by referring to the concept of *ubuntu*. Boraine credits South Africa's ability to come to terms with its past in the way it did to "the holding in balance of the political realities . . . and an ancient philosophy which seeks unity and reconciliation rather than revenge and punishment."[25] The word *ubuntu*—an Nguni word—is a kind of "shorthand" for this "ancient Philosophy." As noted above, it was used deliberately in the Interim Constitution. Boraine goes on to say:

> In reflecting the *ubuntu* philosophy, the Truth and Reconciliation Commission pointed to the need for more community-orientated jurisprudence that acknowledges the reality that individuals are part of a much larger social context.[26]

The concept of *ubuntu* is tied to one's personal identity as we saw earlier and is intrinsic to this "community-orientated" outlook. Desmond Tutu in an interview remarked, "In our understanding, when someone doesn't forgive, we say that person does not have *ubuntu*. That is to say he is not really human."[27] Not to have *ubuntu*—love, forgiveness, generosity—according to both Gyekye and Tutu (and others as well), then, is viewed as a moral deficiency. This is true, in part, because of the context of community in South Africa and the qualities of moral character that flow from this more communitarian way of being.

Of course not all Africans share this moral outlook of black South Africans, nor believe that ethics requires such "supererogatory acts." Tutu remarks: "It doesn't always happen, of course. Where was *ubuntu* in the Belgian Congo in the early 1960's? Why did the Rwandans forget *ubuntu* in 1994 and instead destroy one another in the most awful genocide. . . ? I don't really know except to say that honoring *ubuntu* is clearly not a mechanical, automatic and inevitable process and that we in South Africa have been blessed."[28] The philosophical debate is far from one sided on this issue, and the question of how to bring about reconciliation between parties who had been at war is not an easy one to answer.[29]

The very report of the TRC has its own voice and expresses this concept of *ubuntu* well. It notes first that "individual and shared moral responsibility cannot be adequately addressed by legislation or this commission," but "*what is required is a moral and spiritual renaissance capable of transforming moral indifference, denial, paralyzing guilt and unacknowledged shame, into personal and social responsibility*."[30]

It is in a correlation between *ubuntu*, rooted in whatever forms of "communalism" may survive in South Africa (moderate or otherwise), and the kind of justice referred to as "restorative justice," that we find the foundation stones for the Truth and Reconciliation Commission[31] and a possibility for a moral and spiritual renaissance. In Tutu's own words:

> I contend that there is another kind of justice, restorative justice, which was characteristic of traditional African jurisprudence. Here the central concern is not retribution or punishment but, in the spirit of *ubuntu*, the healing of breaches, the redressing of imbalances, the restoration of broken relationships. This kind of justice seeks to rehabilitate both the victim and the perpetrator, who should be given the opportunity to be reintegrated into the community he or she has injured by his or her offense.[32]

Setting aside whether *ubuntu* is an underlying *elan vital* in "traditional African jurisprudence," it is clear that justice can be conceived in several significantly different ways and one's conception will result in different social consequences. What the TRC has called "restorative justice" does embrace broad goals of "restoring trust" between alienated parties,[33] it evokes an attitude of attention to one's neighbor, and is more likely to enhance goodwill in approaching issues in the rebuilding of a civil society than is "retributive justice."

Another reading of the concept of *ubuntu* tries to keep it free of the burdens of "unanimism." It avoids thinking of *ubuntu* as an ontological concept that applies to all Africans, and it keeps Tutu's question in mind—"why did the Rwandans forget *ubuntu* in 1994?" If we recall our discussion of individual and community in the section on "justice, power, and rights" in chapter 1, Simone Weil and Luce Irigaray argued that "individuals are linked together." They stressed, however, the importance of human obligations to the other, or to one's neighbor—either distant or close. They spoke of community as a "social fabric" woven in such a way as to allow each person to develop their identity by respecting another's dignity and by our connectedness through our obligation to our community. We can think of *ubuntu* as a concept that embodies justice, that underlies human relationships, and that takes precedence over individual "rights." Rather than an ontological concept tied to being African, *ubuntu* is more like an attentive point of view toward one's community, wherein I understand myself as linked with my community. It is true that "being African" may bring about a greater familiarity with this reading of the concept.

Justice may move in a different direction than one of revenge and retribution. The "truth" in the TRC, says Pumla Gobodo-Mandikizela, "was a strategy not only for breaking the cycle of politically motivated violence but also for teaching important lessons about how the human spirit can prevail even as victims remember the cruelty visited upon them in the past."[34] Is not there some *justice in* "breaking the cycle of politically motivated violence" and moving toward a more peaceful and equitable civic order?

Ms. Gobodo-Mandikizela tells of a paper she gave at the First Psychoanalytic Conference in Cape Town in April 1998, where she attempted a psychoanalytic interpretation of her interviews with prisoner Eugene de Kock. She says:

> During the question, a colleague asked whether I had considered the possibility that de Kock was "manipulating" me. I had expected that question and was well prepared for it. But before I could respond, Albie Sachs, a judge on South Africa's Constitutional Court, raised his arm—an arm that had been damaged by a bomb intended to kill him in Mozambique. Instead of answering myself, I called on him. The packed room, filled with psychoanalysts from North America, the United Kingdom, and South Africa, grew hushed. Sachs spoke about how important it was "to see these men's humanity," and how much our hope as South Africans depended on reaching out to such glimpses of humanity in our spirit of compassion instead of revenge. Albie Sachs's words were all the more compelling because, as he spoke, he was gesturing with his cut-off arm.[35]

Is this not an example of *ubuntu*? Does not justice have more to do with the "spirit of compassion instead of revenge"? Should not justice entail moments of hesitation during which we are enabled to view the humanity of our brothers and sisters? *Is not justice inextricably bound up with truth and reconciliation?*

What the TRC may in fact have achieved in terms of its search for truth is a more equitable sense of justice; a sense of justice that embraces reconciliation—a justice that the Commission's formal *Report* calls "restorative justice." The concept of "restorative justice" is not unique to the TRC, but its use by the Commission has helped raise its visibility in legal and ethical debates. We will in Chapter 6 discuss the larger history and contexts of restorative justice and consider it as both an alternative to and complement for the current practices of retributive justice.

One thing that the notion of "restorative justice" did through the TRC was to evoke the importance of transition from a culture of violence—with its gross human rights violations, forced removals and denial of human dignity—to a culture of dignity for all, human rights, and greater public tolerance. The concept of restorative justice also blunts a certain "legalism" found in retributive justice systems that threaten to reduce the concept of justice to one of contentiousness between aggrieved parties. It reminds us that *justice is not simply found in the rule of law but in human social and moral practices that create a civil society,* where all people have equal claim to human dignity and accept responsibility for the well-being of all its citizens. It is this sense of justice that needed to be *restored* in South Africa, and for which the TRC was essentially designed.

Harvard law professor Martha Minow characterized the overall design of the TRC as follows: "On behalf of bystanders and perpetrators, as well as victims, it seeks to establish a base line of right and wrong, to humanize the perpetrators and to obtain and disclose previously hidden information about what happened, who gave orders, where missing persons ended up."[36] If such a baseline is clearly established and the truth is revealed, then the work of national healing and reconciliation might have a place to begin. With such work come new possibilities for a more just society.[37]

To understand the grammar of justice in South Africa one needs first to reveal the truth of apartheid's *injustices*—to confront its acts of injustice, especially among the white ruling community that had become morally bankrupt.[38] This is what is meant by "truth" in the "truth commission." The TRC process is an instance of what Simone Weil called "that halt, that interval of hesitation, wherein lies all our consideration for our brothers in humanity."[39] Such intervals create reflective space, however painful for some and irritating to others, in which new questions could be asked and new risks taken by both victims and perpetrators of violence. In South Africa *attention* needed to be given to the decades of harm done to non-whites by the former white-ruled regime in order for *a new sense of justice* to be restored. Truth-telling was one vehicle for restoring a sense of justice.

What can be argued, and what I am underscoring here, is that *embedded in the TRC process and their Report is the making of a new "moral and spiritual" discourse and the call for a kind of justice called restorative justice that is intended to be the link between "truth" and "reconciliation," and that encourages both moral and social responsibility and such virtues as compassion, mercy and forgiveness, all for the purpose of helping to forge a new and more just South Africa.*

As was noted earlier, it was not a perfect process. For example, the promised monetary reparations that many victims had expected as part of a healing process have only materialized in very small ways, and there is remaining skepticism as to the overall achievement of the Commission's work toward national reconciliation. Even with such disappointment, however, the process produced a remarkable number of dramatic personal acts of reconciliation; each was a visible sign of hope for a society that had suppressed hope for the vast majority of its people, and each can be understood as a new stone laid in a foundation of a justice system serving *all* citizens in the new South Africa.

Part of the Commission's mandate was to recommend reparations for victims and grant amnesty to some perpetrators. The latter was a qualified amnesty provision, that is, amnesty for full disclosure and truth about violations committed and clear evidence that the perpetrators' acts were believed to be politically motivated. This route was chosen rather than one through re-venge or a "Nuremberg-type" tribunal (a retributive or punitive justice model). Such truth disclosure opens up the possibility of thinking about a kind of justice that "aims at moral outcomes," *is compassion-based, embracing human self-esteem, benevolence, and mercy; and a justice grounded in a shared obligation to the well-being of one's fellow human beings*—a well-being that cultivates humanity. But we ask again: what is the relationship of truths revealed in the TRC amnesty hearings to justice?

"The amnesty procedure administered by South Africa's Truth and Reconciliation Commission," writes Ronald Slye (human rights law professor and consultant to the TRC from 1996 to 1998) "was the most sophisticated amnesty undertaken in modern times, if not in any time, for acts that constitute violations of fundamental international human rights."[40] More specifically, writing about the values of the TRC, Kent Greenawalt, university professor at Columbia Law School, says:

> Against worries that raking the coals of past abuse will induce conflict and impede development toward a more just and happy future, powerful reasons exist for exposing the truth. Such exposure allows families and friends of victims to learn what has happened; it provides an official acknowledgment of wrongs; it offers at least a minimal degree of accountability; it may promote psychological healing and reconciliation; it may help discourage similar crimes in the future; *it may assist in reconstituting the moral order, respect for human rights, and the rule of law*; and it may contribute to a "common memory" on which the whole society may build.[41]

Although all these desired ends might not be fully achieved, there has been progress toward them. On the matters of truth revealed and accountability—both necessary for national healing and reconciliation—Slye gives the following assessment: "there is no doubt that the quantity, and probably also the quality, of the information elicited from the amnesty hearings was higher than what would have been elicited from criminal trials."[42] Slye has examined hundreds of transcripts of amnesty hearings and says: "There are few, if any, who can now argue that death squad operations like Vlakpaas did not exist; that people were not tortured; that civilians were not targeted or terrorized. This is so in no small part because some individuals came forward and took responsibility.[43] Slye concludes:

> The South African amnesty process furthered both truth and reconciliation to an extent unprecedented by any previous amnesty agreements. It increased both the quantity and the quality of the information available concerning past violations; and by providing some form of accountability it increased the possibility of cre-

ating a substantive form of reconciliation that would further the creation of a stable democracy protective of human rights.[44]

In South Africa they had to ask would amnesty be within the interest of justice? If one's sense of justice is restorative the answer to the question is Yes!— that is, if you have (or want) a legal system "that aims for moral outcomes" and "societal well-being," then part of that system must have room for forgiveness, pardon, compassion, and mercy—though pardons would not come without much reflection and attention to individual cases. In the new South Africa one clear *moral outcome* desired by the new dispensation *is reconciliation*.[45] Therefore the legal system—to include reconciliation within justice—ought to include mercy. This was shown in its exchange of amnesty for truth (full disclosure of past crimes). This is, in part, what is meant by "restorative justice." Furthermore, by allowing victims the opportunity to tell their stories and (sometimes) receive a sincere apology, the TRC hearings did more for the victims, in general, than retributive justice may have. This, I believe, presents a major challenge to most modern Western conceptions of justice.

There was one process in the Commission's mandate that was designed to achieve greater long-term reconciliation in civil society once the commission officially ended. This was the "institutional hearings." Here the medical, judiciary, business, media, and faith communities, as well as political parties and some NGOs, were asked to testify to the Commission regarding how they had benefited from apartheid, and how they might contribute to the new society's transition to order and economic stability and the overall reconciliation between the white minority culture and the black majority culture. In volume 5, chapter 9 of the *TRC Report* it says: "Reconciliation requires commitment, *especially by those who have benefited and continue to benefit from past discrimination,* to the transformation of unjust inequalities and dehumanizing poverty." Of course the minority economic community under apartheid benefited greatly. Africans were exploited by low wages, dispossessed of their land, had no representation in economic or legislative decisions; there was a vast discrepancy in educational spending between whites and blacks, and blacks had very few, if any, commercial rights to property, pensions, accumulation of wealth and professional development. "Despite our obvious privileging by apartheid," says Wilhelm Verwoerd, "many whites apparently find it difficult to face the facts of being apartheid beneficiaries."[46] The Ugandan scholar, Mahmood Mamdani, based at the University of Cape Town in 1997, argued that the Commission should not have focused on victims and perpetrators, but rather should have shone the spotlight on victims and *beneficiaries* of apartheid. Mamdani wrote:

"Where the focus is on perpetrators, victims are necessarily defined as the minority of political activists; for the victimhood of the majority to be recognized, the focus has to shift from perpetrators to beneficiaries. The difference is this: whereas the focus on perpetrators fuels the demand for justice as criminal justice, that on beneficiaries shifts the focus to a notion of justice as social justice."[47]

Concerns for social justice did come up in the institutional hearings—especially in questioning the business community.[48] In the end, however, Verwoerd notes the near total reluctance of white political and business leaders to take any responsibility for the vast inequities, that he is still "haunted" by an image used by Archbishop Tutu in his foreword to the TRC Report. "The greatest sadness we have encountered in the Commission," Tutu wrote, "has been the reluctance of white leaders to urge their followers to respond to the remarkable generosity of spirit shown by the victims. This reluctance, indeed this hostility, to the Commission has been like spitting in the face of victims."[49] This could be interpreted as an instance of racism shown in the lack of respect of blacks by whites—a lack of recognition of their humanity—it is a truth uncovered by the silence, perhaps an unspoken guilt, of the exposed minority.

The term "mercy" is particularly appropriate to understanding restorative justice because of the reversal of positions of power in the political transition in South Africa, where the preceding white minority regime had little sense of mercy.[50] As cited earlier from Brien, "Mercy provides sight to the moral agent; it enables her to perceive, be sensitive to, and understand the world, and to evaluate the salient moral properties of the people with whom she has contact. This virtue enables an actor to use power wisely."[51] The TRC process seemed to proceed with something like this kind of wisdom, sensing the need to understand the pain of victims and perceive the need that truth must be revealed so as not to bury the past without regret. One could say that as its hearings unfolded it brought a new moral sight to peoples' eyes that enabled them to evaluate human beings in new ways, and to be reminded that power must always be used wisely and with equity and mercy.

Classically, mercy "means restraining the mind from vengeance when it has the power to take it, or the leniency of a superior towards an inferior in fixing punishment."[52] The new majority government certainly had the power to seek vengeance. Remarkably, it did not! Rather it showed mercy through the very process of promoting reconciliation through its Truth Commission. Its leaders had sufficient "moral sight" that enabled them to see and hear the cries of the afflicted. The Commission was clear in its desire to encourage the nation to retain its newly found "moral sight." The Commission *Report* says: "Each story of suffering provided a penetrating window into the past, thereby contributing to a more complete picture of gross violations of human rights in South Africa. The nation must use these stories to sharpen its moral conscience and to ensure that, never again, will it gradually atrophy to the point where personal responsibility is abdicated."[53]

When a final assessment of the TRC is made—and this may be several generations away—it will be said that the notion of "justice" was not left out of their equation of "truth and reconciliation" as many have argued.[54] *Justice comes in through a radical rethinking of the grammar of justice itself and through the process of human restoration that is understood to be as important as, and should become a part of, the rule of law in a time of difficult transition.*

Wilhelm Verwoerd articulates a clear achievement of the TRC: "From the perspective of 'restorative justice,' the TRC is not a 'second-best option' but a contribution to a different, more complete kind of justice."[55] On this point we have linked the concept of restorative justice with Seneca's idea of thoroughly examining "the circumstances of human life." The TRC has pointed to one way of "cultivating humanity" and provided us with both an historical and imaginative moral narrative to examine our humanity and find ways to avoid our inhumanity in the future. We shall, in Chapter 6, return to the larger notion of "restorative justice" and look at some specific examples of reconciliation that emerged from the TRC process, and we will take a closer look at some of the more formal aspects and the multiple sides of "restorative justice" in cross-cultural perspective.

NOTES

1. Andrew Brien, "Mercy Within Legal Justice," *Social Theory and Practice* 24, no. 1 (Spring 1998): 104f.
2. Brien, "Mercy Within Legal Justice," 106.
3. Nussbaum, *Sex and Social Justice*, 161.
4. Nussbaum, *Sex and Social Justice*, 166.
5. Nussbaum, *Sex and Social Justice*, 166.
6. As found in Jonathan Sacks, *The Dignity of Difference: How to Avoid the Clash of Civilizations* (London, New York: Continuum, 2003), 182. Sacks' overall discussion of mercy and forgiveness is a very interesting one in the context of biblical Judaism. See his chapter 10: "Conciliation: The Power of a Word to Change the World."
7. Simone Weil, *The Need for Roots,* 40. My emphasis.
8. Simone Weil, *Selected Essays,* 30.
9. Simone Weil, *Gravity and Grace,* 121.
10. Simone Weil, *The Need for Roots,* 121.
11. Ronald K. L. Collins and Finn E. Nielsen, "The Spirit of Simone Weil's Law," found in *Simone Weil's Philosophy of Culture* ed. Richard H. Bell (1993), and Richard H. Bell, *Simone Weil: The Way of Justice as Compassion* (1998), 217–242. Selections taken from *Simone Weil: The Way of Justice as Compassion*, 236–238.

12. Pumla Gobodo-Mandikizela, *A Human Being Died That Night: A South African Story of Forgiveness* (Boston and New York: Houghton Mifflin Co., 2003), 126.

13. The commission was legislated into being by the National Unity and Reconciliation Act (No. 34 of 1995).

14. The idea of the TRC as a national "imaginative narrative" can be plainly seen by reading the 1998 Report of the TRC and the account of its unfolding process as told by Antjie Krog in her prize-winning book *Country of My Skull* (1998).

15. For some in the audience, acts of forgiveness were linked more with pity and humiliation for perpetrators of crimes than they were to merciful acts tied to justice. Also to uncover some heinous act carried out by the state seemed closer to scapegoating than it did to a pursuit of justice.

16. Senghor was a poet/philosopher and the liberation leader of the Senegalese people against French colonial rule of his native land, Senegal.

17. Soyinka, *The Burden of Memory*, especially Chapter 2, "L. S. Senghor and Negritude," 1999.

18. Soyinka, "The Past Must Address Its Present," in *Wole Soyinka: An Appraisal*, ed. Adewale Maja-Pearce (Oxford: Heinemann Educational Publishers, 1994), 19.

19. See Alex Boraine, *A Country Unmasked: Inside South Africa's Truth and Reconciliation Commission* (Oxford: Oxford University Press, 2000), 425.

20. Gyekye, *Tradition and Modernity: Philosophical Reflections on the African Experience* (New York and Oxford: Oxford University Press, 1997), 73.

21. Gyekye, *Tradition and Modernity*, 73.

22. Joe Slovo is associated with introducing the "sunset clause" that would enable the National Party government to share in power during the first few years of majority rule. Cf. Waldmeir, *Anatomy*, pp. 213–15, 222. Kadar Asmal perhaps deserves most credit for shaping the idea of a Truth and Reconciliation Commission that originated out of the ANC. See Boraine, *A Country Unmasked*, 12–14, 260. There were many non-black leaders (whites and South Africans of Indian and Malay descent) besides Slovo, of course, who actively fought against apartheid and whose supererogatory acts helped in the freedom struggle and social transition process.

23. Nelson Mandela, *Long Walk to Freedom*, 544.

24. This is not to say that Mandela was not engaged in "politics" and that this entails mixed motivation. I think, however, there is little doubt that Mandela's "politics" were moderated by his "ethics," and that the well-being of *all* South Africans was always part of his political vision. This is confirmed by Alex Boraine when he says of Mandela: "From the day of his release to the present time, he has focused on the need to come to terms with the past, but always with a readiness to forgive and to move on. . . . He stretched out a hand of reconciliation and friendship." Boraine, *A Country Unmasked*, 261, 362.

There are recent studies of the South African concept of *ubuntu* that link it both to Mandela's Xhosa upbringing and to Tutu's Christian theology. See William I . Zartman, *Traditional Cures for Modern Conflicts* (London: Lynne Rienner Publishers, 2000). Zartman says, for example, that in Xhosa society, "*ubuntu* is an expression of our collective personhood and invokes images of group support, acceptance, co-operation, care and solidarity" (170). *Ubuntu* is linked to Tutu's Christian theology in Michael Battle, *The Ubuntu Theology of Desmond Tutu* (Cleveland, OH: The Pilgrim Press, 1997).

25. Boraine, *A Country Unmasked*, 423.

26. Boraine, *A Country Unmasked*, p. 425.

27. Waldmeir, *Anatomy*, 268. Tutu says the same of *ubuntu* in his book *No Future without Forgiveness*, 34–36.

28. Desmond Tutu, *No Future without Forgiveness*, 36.

29. For broad and insightful discussions of the relationship of vengeance and forgiveness and of the relationship of truth commissions to justice in the wake of the "mass atrocities" of this century, see Martha Minow, *Between Vengeance and Forgiveness: Facing History after Genocide and Mass Violence*, foreword by Judge Richard J. Goldstone (Boston: Beacon Press, 1998), and Priscilla B. Hayner, *Unspeakable Truths* (New York and London: Routledge, 2001).

For a severely realistic, if not overly grim, look at the extent of division between black and white and among rival black groups in South Africa, read the brutally honest account of apartheid evils and the possibility or impossibility of reconciliation in Rian Malan's *My Traitor's Heart* (London: Vintage, 1991). This gives one a clear view of just how intractable the South African transition would seem and gives one an appreciation for the sense of balance struck between the political realities and a desire for unity and reconciliation.

30. *Report of the Truth and Reconciliation Commission*, vol. 1/5, section 103. My emphasis.

31. The concept of "restorative justice" is inscribed in the *TRC Report*. See vol. I, chapter 5.

32. Tutu, *No Future Without Forgiveness*, 51f.

33. Trudy Govier and Wilhelm Verwoerd draw attention to "trust" in discussing various meanings of reconciliation. Reconciliation can be seen as an instrument that supports movement toward a just society—an instrument for the building or rebuilding of trust, especially between large social groups "in the aftermath of alienation or tension." Govier and Verwoerd, "Trust and the Problem of National Reconciliation," unpublished essay, 5.

34. Pumla Gobodo-Mandikizela, *A Human Being Died*, 103.

35. Pumla Gobodo-Mandikizela, *A Human Being Died*, 45.

36. Minow, *Between Vengeance and Forgiveness: Facing History after Genocide and Mass Violence* (Boston: Beacon Press, 1998), 78. See also de Lange, "The Historical Context, Legal Origins and Philosophical Foundation of the South African Truth and Reconciliation Commission." in *Looking Back Reaching Forward* eds. Villa-Vicencio and Verwoerd (Cape Town: University of Cape Town Press, Zed Books Ltd., London, 2000), esp. 22–26.

37. In a comparative study of the Truth Commissions of the past thirty years, Priscilla Hayner cites the results of the Truth Commissions of Argentina (1983–1984), Chile (1990–1991), and El Salvador (1992–1993) that directly affected the reform of the legal justice systems of those countries, making them more accountable to the

public. Priscilla Hayner, *Unspeakable Truths: Confronting State Terror and Atrocity* (New York and London, Routledge, 2001).

38. The African National Congress (the anti-apartheid party) partially faced up to its own injustices during the last years of the struggle by convening two Truth Commissions—one in 1992 and one in 1993, to deal with human rights violations inflicted on its own members and to prisoners it held during the struggle. See Hayner, *Unspeakable Truths*, 60f.

39. Simone Weil, *The Iliad*, 14. Simone Weil was referring to the grieving wives and widows in the *Iliad* at the time their loved ones were dying in war "far from hot baths." The grieving gives all pause for reflection about what has gone terribly wrong.

40. Ronald C. Slye, "Amnesty, Truth, and Reconciliation," in *Truth V. Justice: The Morality of Truth Commission,* ed. R. I. Rothberg and D. Thompson (Princeton and Oxford: Princeton University Press, 2002), 171.

41. Greenawalt, "Amnesty's Justice" in *Truth V. Justice,* ed. Rosenberg and Thompson, 189. My emphasis.

42. Slye, *Truth V. Justice,* 177.

43. Slye, *Truth V. Justice,* 181f.

44. Slye, *Truth V. Justice,* 183. Priscilla Hayner gives a very compelling example of how one particular set of amnesty hearings, packed with hundreds of angry people at Richards Bay, led to a major reconciliation between the members of the Inkatha Freedom Party who were seeking amnesty and families of murdered African National Congress members. This was a case of what was called "black on black violence." These hearings ended with a complete turnaround of attitudes. Hayner notes the following: "one by one survivors came forward and forgave the applicants and thanked them for telling everything, allowing them to know what had happened and also telling them what else had been involved and who had given instructions. At the end of the meeting a resolution was taken to forgive the applicants and to tell the committee that the community accepted that the applicants were telling the whole truth within the bounds of the failings of human memory . . . they would not oppose amnesty. . . . At the end of the meeting people rushed forward to hug the applicants." [Hayner, *Unspeakable Truths,* 158]

Another point to be noted is that of some 7,000 applicants processed for amnesty, amnesty was granted to just over 20 percent of the applicants. This was, in part, due to amnesty seekers *not telling the truth.* Those not granted amnesty may still be subject to civil and criminal trials in the state justice system.

45. See vol. 1/5, sections 10–28 of the *Report*, "Promoting National Unity and Reconciliation."

46. Wilhelm Verwoerd, "The TRC and Apartheid Beneficiaries in a News Dispensation," published by the Centre for the Study of Violence and Reconciliation, January 19, 2003, 2. See also the excellent article by Sampie Terreblanche, "Dealing with Systematic Economic Injustice," in *Looking Back Reaching Forward,* ed. Charles Villa-Vicencio and Wilhelm Verwoerd, 265–276.

47. As found in Hayner, *Unspeakable Truths,* 164. In another essay of Mamdani's on the TRC, he concluded that the "truth" in the commission was "A diminished truth." See his "A Diminished Truth," *Siyaya!* Issue 3 (Spring 1998): 38–40.

48. See essay by Terreblanche, "Dealing with Systematic Economic Injustice."

49. Verwoerd, "The TRC and Apartheid Beneficiaries," 3.

50. Within the "merciless" framework of apartheid, there were, of course, individual acts of mercy shown to victims by persons who were members of the power structure. Some of these came out in the public hearings and show the meaning and value of reconciliation. See the case of "the angel of mercy" Irene Crouse in her acts of kindness to the tortured Ivy Gcina. *Report*, 5, no. 9, sections 66–69.

51. Andrew Brien, "Mercy Within Legal Justice," 104.

52. Andrew Brien, "Mercy Within Legal Justice," 18f. This is the definition given by Seneca in the *De Clementia,* and Brien goes on to discuss the dynamics of "power and vulnerability . . . in which an act of mercy occurs." 84.

53. *Report*, 1/5, section 109.

54. The South African Institute of Race Relations, Johannesburg, wrote a seriously critical assessment of some of the commissions shortcomings—especially as communicated in its 1998 *Report*. See Anthea Jeffery, *The Truth about the Truth Commission* (1999).

Even now, however, seven years or more since this evaluation, a number of penetrating studies of the Commission's ongoing effect on individuals and South African Society have appeared that confirm its overall positive impact. See the documentary film, "Long Night's Journey into Day"; John W. de Gruchy, *Reconciliation: Restoring Justice* (Minneapolis, MN: Fortress Press, 2002), especially Part Three; Gobodo-Mandikizela, *A Human Being Died That Night*; and Alec Boraine, *A Country Unmasked: Inside South Africa's Truth and Reconciliation Commission* (Oxford: Oxford University Press, 2000), see especially chapters 8 through 11.

55. Verwoerd, "Individual and/or Social Justice after Apartheid?" *The European Journal of Development Research* 11, no. 2, (December 1999): 124.

Chapter Four

Justice Across Boundaries I: The Moral and Literary Imagination

"One may . . . observe in one's travels to distant countries the feelings of recognition and affiliation that link every human being to every other human being."

[Aristotle, *Nichomachean Ethics*, 1155a–20]

SYMPATHETIC UNDERSTANDING

We have seen how the overcoming of obstacles can be understood as both (a) an ordinary condition of life that human beings regularly navigate with their fellow human beings as they "read" each other and (b) an overwhelming task if life's circumstances have conspired to place burdens and injustices at every path of one's life. While we know "mercy in legal justice" may apply to offenders who stand before a judge and mitigating circumstances may call for lenient punishment for crimes, there are literally millions of human beings who commit no crimes but whose life's circumstances lead us to more than a "merciful attitude" or pity toward them. We say of these "millions" they are "owed" more in life. A conservative response may be to ask: "Who owes them more? I may pity their circumstances, but I owe them nothing for I am not responsible for their circumstances." Another response to this is to say: "Well, perhaps! But *their* society or state may owe them something and should provide a decent basic human life for them. I, however, am not a part of that society or state. In *my* state we have certain 'welfare' provisions—a 'safety net' so to speak— that provides for those whose circumstances were 'unfortunate.'" We may attribute such circumstances of life that millions suffer to poverty, famine,

67

wars, disease, or unjust oppression, and that these problems are for respective governments to solve. With such a response before us it is a long struggle to think about the idea of justice across boundaries.[1] It is not an easy task to convince human beings that it is "our" responsibility to care for humanity, and even more, that we each (all of us) have *an obligation to care*. It is just this extent of caring that justice demands in our world today. How is such an understanding evoked?

Martha Nussbaum provides us with another classical clue to arousing such an understanding. She notes that Aristotle uses the word *suggnome*, or "judging with," that can lead to "a forgiving attitude to 'human things.'" Aristotle links *suggnome* closely with sympathy or compassion, "an attitude he defines as requiring the thought that one's own possibilities are in significant ways shared with those of the person one contemplates, and that this person was overwhelmed by obstacles not of his own making."[2] Colloquially we might think of the phrase: "There, but for the grace of God, go I." In this way one may come to share the other person's point of view and move toward or perhaps even beyond some sympathetic understanding. This attitude stands in opposition to either a "neutral" attitude or a "revenge-taking" attitude. This attitude of sympathy or compassion was often seen in reactions to the testimonies and stories told by both victims and perpetrators during the many months of the South African TRC public hearings. One could argue that this was often done in sympathetic response to another human being. It even led in numerous cases to victims forgiving those who did terrible things to them or to loved ones and who sought forgiveness.

Wittgenstein had also seen this problem in his reflections on how we could come to understand the practices of people in a "strange country" and commented that we must learn how to "find ourselves in the other." This requires finding a way to get closer to the "character" and "spirit" of the people you cannot understand. He says that in approaching another's day-to-day moral and social practices we in turn must find the room in ourselves to see connections, new aspects of the other's life with our own, and possible appropriations of those practices in our life. The understanding passes both ways in the seeing. Wittgenstein calls this an *"ubersichtliche" Darstellung*. This way of seeing leads to the possibility of mutual recognition and seeing things as a whole.[3] How are we to bring ourselves closer to the stranger? How are we to be led to the possibility of such mutual recognition?

Here is where we can return to the suggestive nature found in the work of Hallie, Gaita, and Glover in their attempts to arouse our "moral imagination." They do this by *looking at the face of harmdoing and evil in history* and in seeing our humanity through it all. Or we can focus attention on our "literary imagination" to reveal a similar sympathetic understanding toward the other.

Let us turn to these two "imaginative" paths. Our first step will be to look at some moral-historical examples and second to some literary examples.

THE MORAL IMAGINATION

There are few relatively unambiguous examples of truly good people who have navigated the seas of moral ambiguity with courage and clarity, who show goodness and justice in human affairs. When an example does come to light, it shows all the marks of what Simone Weil calls "the madness of love." One thinks of extraordinary people like Mahatma Gandhi or Dorothy Day or Mother Teresa of Calcutta or Martin Luther King Jr., or Nelson Mandela or Vaclav Havel. There are also moving examples shown through the lives of *ordinary people*. One such example is found in the story of the people of the French Huguenot village of Le Chambon-sur-Lignon who, during World War II, placed themselves at risk out of gratitude to God and in unconditional love to save the lives of Jewish children.[4] They did so on their own accord, guided by their traditional religious aspirations and what Hallie called the "mysterious virtues" of compassion and generosity. Their action was motivated by others' suffering. They were witness to what they believed to be an obligation to help others in need. It is ironic that while Simone Weil was talking about "mad love" and desperately trying to find a way to practice it in her war-torn homeland while being exiled in London, the people of Le Chambon were "madly" at work loving those most afflicted—Jewish children fleeing from certain death. The example set at this time in Le Chambon is precisely the kind of pure expression of sympathetic understanding and justice infused with love needed to spur our moral imaginations. It was also a display of justice across boundaries—national boundaries, ethnic boundaries, and religious boundaries.[5]

In his story about Le Chambon, Hallie tries to get to the root of "how goodness happened there." He is particularly drawn to Magda Trocmé, wife of the community's charismatic pastor and leader, André Trocmé. Magda's goodness seems unusually pure and unencumbered by ethical theory. In *Lest Innocent Blood Be Shed*, the story of the whole village is told and a number of good people are discussed, while in his follow-up book, *In the Eye of the Hurricane: Tales of Good and Evil, Help and Harm*, Hallie focuses on Magda's goodness. Magda seemed to understand the responsibility one has when one faces another human being. Hallie puts it this way: "Magda Trocmé believes that something is evil because it *hurts* people. Hers is an ethic of benevolence; she needed only to look into the eyes of a refugee in order to find her duty."[6] She immediately understood the depth that goes with each human being and the mutual respect that this commands. It was this "automatic" pattern of helping that drew Hallie to uncover the story of Le Chambon.

In *Tales*, Hallie draws a comparison of the ambiguities found in twentieth-century morality to Goethe's Faust. Faust had two souls in one body, each wanting to tear itself away from the other. Hallie sees in himself a human torn between these two souls, living two distinct kinds of virtues. The first kind of virtue grows from acting in terms of one's own self-interest and preservation; it "rests on the sound biological and psychological bedrock of self-preservation."[7] Of this kind there are what he calls "little virtues" like thrift and caution; "they protect our hides" and are commonsensical—reasonable ways of behaving in order to preserve our lives and comforts. The second kind of virtue includes "mysterious" actions, one's "motivated by another person's needs"—"you are not the center; the helped person is." This virtue is expressed in compassion and generosity. This seems both impractical and "unnatural," but to the Chambonnais, especially to Magda, exercising a "mysterious" virtue became an ordinary, natural practice as they went about welcoming strangers and saving lives. Magda embodied what St. Benedict in his *Rule for Monasteries* would call a welcoming attitude. We see in this attitude the embodiment of human respect, a natural regard for the dignity of every human being—these are part of our humanity and a necessary component in our rethinking of justice.

Singlemindedness in the service of others, or "recklessness" concerned only with a sufferer, is another way of understanding this goodness in human affairs—where compassion and generosity appear completely selfless. Hallie provides another tale of such goodness. The "saint" of this story is Joshua James, the nineteenth-century patron saint of the U.S. Life Saving Service (later to become the Search and Rescue arm of the U.S. Coast Guard), and his "surfmen" and fellow villagers of Hull, Massachusetts. He and his fellow villagers embodied the virtues of "benevolence, hospitality and helpfulness." What Hallie discovered in this "immovably centered" man was a goodness that was visible in the form of his being—in what he did to save lives for almost sixty years.[8] "His power to spread life," says Hallie, "did not lie in one of his deeds, like what he did in the storm of '88. It was his whole persistent, centered, life-giving life that was the very *form* and essence of [his] decency."[9] "Moral beauty happens," concludes Hallie, "when someone carves out a place for compassion in a largely ruthless universe. It happened in the French village of Le Chambon during the war, and it happened in and near the American village of Hull during the long lifetime of Joshua James."[10]

Raimond Gaita provides us with a very different kind of moral example. In trying to understand the meaning of the Holocaust, the very concepts of suffering and injustice of such proportion stand as major stumbling blocks to the idea supposedly generated by the Enlightenment of human moral progress in the West. Even though the Nuremburg Tribunals coined a new and important phrase that entered our modern moral and legal vocabulary, "crimes against humanity," Gaita says that the Nazi crimes against the Jews were, in fact, more than that. They were not just one such terrible crime against humanity that all genocidal acts are. Rather, the Holocaust is uniquely evil. To distinguish the Holocaust from other terrible acts against humanity has proven to be very difficult and not everyone agrees with this view. Gaita, however, makes a stab at identifying its distinctiveness. He says: "the Holocaust did not merely crush the hopes of continuous human progress, the hopes of the enlightenment. It did so in ways that put in doubt our understanding of ourselves as moral and political beings."[11]

After reading Primo Levi's book *If This Is a Man* (a work Gaita says is "one of the great spiritual achievements of human kind"), Gaita remarks that it became apparent to those in the Warsaw Ghetto as they began receiving news of the "massive and unrelenting scale of the killings in the east" that something different and *more terrible in kind* had begun. He continues:

> Some people realized what was really being done in the ghettos when they heard of the killings in the [death camps in the] east. . . . In the east the Nazis' genocidal purpose became transparent. In the death camps . . . something even more terrible than genocide was being committed. The death camps are essential to our understanding of the Holocaust, not because they were horrifically efficient killing centers, but because there occurred in them an assault on the preciousness of individual human beings of a kind never seen before. That, I think, is the truth in Avishai Margalit's claim that the Holocaust was unique because it combined mass murder with demonic efforts to humiliate those who were destined to be murdered.[12]

What we are led to imagine is an assault on the meaning of what it is to be a human being; the total disregard plus the humiliation of human dignity; a racism that crossed known moral boundaries and neutralized all possibility of sympathetic understanding on the part of the Nazis with regard to a Jew. There was no meaningful way of using the moral concept of "respect" much less, "mutual respect." To the Nazis there was *no "other" to face*!

Another historical example that challenges our moral imagination is found in Glover's account of the Cuban missile crisis. There are several aspects in the unfolding of the Cuban missile crisis in October of 1962 that bear on our rethinking of justice. The one aspect I want to briefly discuss (that Glover brings to our attention) is *the moral tone* found in the resolution of the crisis. This is seen primarily in the words and actions of the Soviet president Nikita Khrushchev, President John F. Kennedy, Robert Kennedy, and U.S. Secretary

of State Dean Rusk. The very first decision made by President Kennedy—
against the advice of his military advisors who wanted to go immediately into
Cuba and take out all the missile bases—was to blockade Soviet ships from
bringing any more offensive or defensive weapons into Cuba. Of this decision President Kennedy said: "we don't want to push him [Khrushchev] to a
precipitous action—*give him time to consider.* I don't want him put in a
corner from which he cannot escape."[13] Glover notes that both Heads of State,
Presidents Kennedy and Khrushchev, "were emotionally responsive to [the]
enormity [of the crisis and its potential dark consequences]."[14] Any decision
or set of decisions taken were not a simple result of "rational" calculation.
One had to think about the consequences of possible nuclear war. President
Kennedy and Dean Rusk had, upon coming to office, been briefed on such
consequences and given a scenario of some 200 million dead, and Robert
Kennedy estimated that had the Soviets unleashed their missiles on the
United States it would kill 80 million Americans. The risk was too large! On
the other side, Khrushchev's experiences in two world wars was revealed in
his first letter [or formal response] to President Kennedy during the early days
of the crisis—a letter Glover notes that "had a conciliatory and human tone."
This letter, some argue, had "changed the atmosphere" from one of anger to
one of a willingness to listen, to not over react, and to compromise. Part of
this letter reads as follows:

> Should war indeed break out, it would not be in our power to contain or stop it,
> for such is the logic of war. I have taken part in two wars, and I know that war
> ends only when it has rolled through cities and villages, sowing death and de-
> struction everywhere. . . . If people do not display wisdom, they will eventually
> reach the point where they will clash, like blind moles, and then mutual annihi-
> lation will commence. . . . You and I should not now pull on the ends of the rope
> in which you have tied a knot of war, because the harder you and I pull, the
> tighter this knot will become. And a time may come when this knot is tied so
> tight that the person who tied it is no longer capable of untying it, and then the
> knot will have to be cut.[15]

Neither leader wanted to pull the knot in the rope too tightly. Both of their
memories of being in war, and President Kennedy and Dean Rusk having
learned from reading of mistakes that led to World War I in Barbara Tuch-
man's book, *The Guns of August*, helped defuse the crisis. Robert Kennedy
sums up this "emotionally responsive" reaction as follows: "We spent more
time on [the] moral questions during the first five days than on any other single matter. . . . We struggled and fought with one another and with our consciences, for it was a question that deeply troubled us all."[16] After the crisis

Khrushchev wrote to President Kennedy that "we had to step over our pride, both you and we, in order to reach this agreement."[17]

Note the number of cues that caused "a halt" in this episode—those "intervals of hesitation, wherein lies all our consideration for our brothers in humanity":

- "give him time to consider"
- "display wisdom"
- a "human tone"
- avoidance of "sowing death and destruction everywhere"
- "emotionally responsive"
- "step over our pride"

These are vivid images for our imagination to grasp; reminding us, again, that the moral and political dimensions of life are intertwined. If, as we have argued earlier, an end of justice is to aim at moral outcomes, then the concepts of trust, hesitation, and attention, and consideration of the humanity of the other can never be left out of the meaning of justice itself.

Following these images of war and the prospect of attention to human suffering—of "sowing death and destruction everywhere" and an appropriate "display of wisdom"—we find another, more contemporary example dramatically expressed in a tone of remorse, even despair, from the assassin Eugene de Kock, known as "Prime Evil" during the waning years of apartheid and during the TRC hearings. De Kock told Pumla Gobodo-Mandikizela in one of her many interviews with him in prison:

> I think that I lost—it's a feeling of loss. Well, the first thing that goes is innocence, I mean, there's no more fairy tales and Bambi. That is gone. We killed a lot of people, they killed some of ours. We fought for nothing, we fought each other basically eventually for nothing. We could have all been alive having a beer. And the politicians? If we could put all politicians in the front lines with their families, and grandparents, and grandchildren—if they are in the front line, I don't think we will ever have a war again. I think it's educated people, very educated people, who sit in parliament and decide about war. So I am confused, I am just very tired.[18]

"We struggled and fought with one another and with our consciences," said Robert Kennedy. Perhaps we are "too educated" to avoid injustice; perhaps we should be sitting around a table "having a beer."

There are, of course, scores of instructive examples in history that move our moral imagination. The books from which the above examples are drawn have numerous additional examples and each of us could enhance the list with our own favorite "stories of good and evil."

THE LITERARY IMAGINATION

A second path to opening up our imaginative capacities to rethinking justice across boundaries is through the literature and art of a culture or country. Nussbaum writes, referring to one such piece of fiction: Andrea Dworkin's novel *Mercy.* "The novel's structure," says Nussbaum, "is a structure of *suggnome*—of the penetration of the life of another into one's own imagination and heart. It is a form of imaginative and emotional receptivity, in which the reader, following the author's lead, comes to be inhabited by the tangled complexities and struggles of other concrete lives."[19] I will turn now to a few literary examples that have this same capacity to evoke our imaginations toward greater "emotional receptivity" and sympathetic understanding in us and toward strangers in distant lands and cultures.

Part of seeing the other and their particular life circumstances is enhanced through the literary imagination, or more generally through what I call an aesthetic consciousness. I may not have firsthand awareness of the other's circumstances, but can come to a more sympathetic understanding of them as narrated through their stories, novels, local ritual dramas, or iconic forms of art. Part of the narrative consciousness of a culture is its aesthetic consciousness. An aesthetic consciousness orders sensible experience in both a factual and an imaginative way to express human hope and wholeness. When a work of art is produced from the aesthetic consciousness and displays, for example, only the fractured, disorienting, and suffering nature of human life, it is making a judgment on the culture that is itself fractured and hurting, pointing to the incompleteness of human life. In its literature, its art, its stories we visually see something of that incompleteness.[20] In the seeing, the truths of the human situation are revealed.

To bring this idea into focus, I will look at a few literary examples from the African context to help us think more clearly about justice across boundaries. The point of departure of an African's *seeing* of her world may be different from my own. Both the inherited background (the social history surrounding the slave trade and manifest forms of colonialism, the state of present suffering and poverty) and the post-colonial reality that shapes Africa's current social and moral environment must be made accessible to me if I am to claim a sympathetic understanding of it. There must be ways in which I can listen to and hear the many voices of Africa and connect them up with my own understanding. As Edward Said wrote: "Stories are at the heart of what explorers and novelists say about strange regions of the world; they also become the method colonized people use to assert their own identity and the existence of their own history."[21] We share in forming and expressing our particular life-worlds through our narratives—that is common to our humanity.

Awareness of the condition of great suffering and the struggle to overcome it for all the reasons given and more has also been characterized by a new theme running through more recent African literature, generating what Kwame Anthony Appiah calls a "second stage" of the African novel. The "first stage" comprised of works like Achebe's *Things Fall Apart*, Laye's *L'Enfant noir*, Kane's *Ambiguous Adventure,* and Sembene's, *God's Bits of Wood* focused on issues like exile and African "identity" based on nationalism or negritude and anti-colonial liberation from the "Western Imperium." Appiah says of these: "The novels of this first stage are thus realist legitimations of nationalism: they authorize a 'return to traditions' while at the same time recognizing the demands of a Weberian rationalized modernity."[22]

A second stage in the African novel, particularly francophone novels of the later 1960s and 1970s, are motivated by the growing awareness that nationalism was failing, and governments had lost their legitimacy. The second stage, says Appiah, is based on an appeal to ethical universals—"it is based, as intellectual responses to oppression in Africa largely are based, in an appeal to a certain *simple respect for human suffering*, a fundamental revolt against the endless misery of the last thirty years."[23] There is an emphasis here of both hopelessness and compassion. An emphasis is turned toward *the people* not the nation and to the alleviation of day-to-day suffering. Solidarity with human suffering becomes a sign of what it means to be African. The whole sense of what it means to be an African is fragmented and confused in the post-colonial mind; hope is found only in and with the suffering and compassion of all who are victimized. It is in both this fragmentation and the hope that the idea of justice surfaces in the struggle for transformation in numerous present-day African societies. In these later novels there surfaces an embedded sense of both despair and compassion, even if sometimes cynically molded into a novel's characters, rejecting nationalistic rhetoric for a basic *humanism*. But even that humanism seems buried. The deep sense of loss, an overwhelming sense of evil cries out to be heard. Examples of these post-colonial novels are Yambo Ouologuem's *Le Devoir de Violence*, and V. Y. Mudimbe's *L'Ecart* and *Entre les eaux*.

In this sense of human suffering—the crying out to be heard—this fiction is another example where engagement with Africa is a two-way path; where the quality of the ideas are so compelling as to make non-Africans turn their heads, listen, and examine their own lives. Learning to listen in this way to Africa's suffering, then, is the starting point of a meaningful comparative ethics and an inroad to greater sympathetic understanding; it is a way toward finding justice across boundaries.

A similar sense of despair and suffering comes through novels and short stories out of southern Africa in the past thirty years. The apartheid era, for example, created an "ethos of remorselessness," especially among white Afrikaners, said philosopher Johan Snyman.[24] There was a huge gap in the perception of what is right and wrong. It was only as South African perpetrators of heinous crimes applied for amnesty and began their testimonies through the TRC process that awareness of this gap began to dawn on the white culture. Snyman discusses the work of Antjie Krog, *Country of My Skull*, as an appropriate summary of Afrikaners coming to terms with their suppression of a moral discourse to deal with the injustice of apartheid and the great suffering it caused. On the other side, black literature, some written by South Africans in exile, not only narrates the great suffering and injustices of apartheid, but also gives voice to the struggles facing blacks in the daily circumstances of life.

A good example of black struggles is found in Sindiwe Magona's *Mother to Mother*, a novel that gives voice to the mother of the young man who fatally stabbed the young American woman, Amy Biehl, in a black township of Cape Town. This African mother addresses Amy Biehl's mother. Here you have the story of growing up in the last decade or so of the apartheid regime and how it caused so many to lose their moral way in both white and black communities. This story, though a fictional account, was part of what led the Biehls to forgive their daughter's killer and set up a foundation to promote reconciliation in the new South Africa. This book and its actual response from the Biehls is a wonderful example of the working of *suggnome* or "emotional receptivity" and learning to "judge with" another.[25] This example and others like it help to lay a foundation for a new kind of justice as reconciliation in the new South Africa.

The novels and short stories of Bessie Head deal mostly with the earlier years of apartheid and the ways in which the majority of southern Africans (particularly in Botswana) survive scarcity and oppression. Head narrates how living in simple ways grows out of their traditions and mutual reliance on one another. Author Bessie Head calls herself a "dreamer and storyteller." She says of those who dream and tell stories that they "have seen life" at eye level and are "drunk with the magical enchantment of human relationships," and she notes that one "always welcome[s] the storyteller." And what do such dreamers and storytellers provide for us? "Each human society," she says, "is a narrow world, trapped to death in paltry evils and jealousies, and for people to know that there are thoughts and generosities wider and freer than their own can only be an enrichment to their lives."[26]

Storytellers, with their pictures and narratives [both oral and written], enrich our lives beyond our own narrow world and help us understand the other's world. Thus I can see something of southern Africa through the stories of Bessie Head, and also something of *my* familiar narrow world in the southern United States, with its "paltry evils and jealousies," through stories of Flannery O'Connor or William Faulkner. In these stories we can enrich each other's lives.

Head's stories tell of human innocence and the individual desires of women and men to neutralize evil and to love beyond and grow beyond their traditional village customs of arranged marriages, clan struggles, and communal taboos.[27] She writes of the dignity found in poverty and humility— African virtues born of circumstances, and virtues that free a human being for forgiveness and hope.

The poverty of which Head speaks is partly imposed by colonial invaders. She writes: "thieves had stolen the land and were so anxious to cover up all traces of the theft that correspondingly, all traces of the true history have been obliterated. We, as black people, could make no appraisal of our own worth; we did not know who or what we were, apart from objects of abuse and exploitation."[28] Her works are portraits of the recovery of human worth and dignity. South African literary critic Annie Gagiano says of Head's novel *A Bewitched Crossroad—An African Saga*, that it can be read as a major act of reclamation. "It is a text which works throughout by recognizing all those rights and dignities which were denied by the colonial sneer and the settler's brutal greed."[29] Head was determined not to glamorize the black African, but rather "to insist on the deep human worth of the actual people and the need to portray their lives accurately."[30] Head wrote of the need to "[reclaim] that humility that has been trampled on and abused."[31] In *A Bewitched Crossroad*, and other works, power was recast in forms of compassion and dignity; her characters used power and powerlessness to humanize society.

This "unconscious dignity" among Africans is linked to their desire to avoid evil, whether by "spells" or "medicines," or by the avoidance of violence, or by accommodation to circumstances. Bessie Head's story "The Power Struggle," about the avoidance of evil and the maintenance of dignity begins:

The universe had a more beautiful dream. It was not the law of the jungle or the survival of the fittest but a dream that had often been the priority of Saints—the power to make evil irrelevant. All the people of southern Africa had lived out this dream before the dawn of the colonial era. Time and again it sheds its beam of light on their affairs although the same patterns of horror would arise like dark engulfing waves.[32]

The picture/story then painted/told of two brothers Davhana and Baeli and their rival struggle for power is a story of good and evil. The way this story is presented has an interesting parallel to Kierkegaard's account of the parable of Jesus at the house of Simon the Pharisee [Luke 7: 36–50] when an unnamed woman bursts in and weeps and anoints Jesus' feet with oil. Kierkegaard notes that the woman says nothing, that "she is what she does not say. . . she *is* a characterization, like a picture: she has. . . forgotten herself, she, the lost one, who is now lost in her Savior, lost in him as she rests at his feet—like a picture."[33]

Davhana, the symbol of the good, is also "like a picture" lost in life, forced to choose goodness over evil, peace over violence, life over power. It is his silent dignity that helps him avoid intrigue, and his actions to avoid evil are *his* "characterization." We *see* Davhana, like a picture, and react to what we see. He frees himself from burdens of power, like a child, to maintain a sense of innocence. It is such pictures that give us pleasure and cast a "beam of light" on goodness rather than evil, thus keeping a dream alive.

In our reaction to such stories we have "made room for" aspects of Africa's vision; we have allowed Africa to come to us. In doing this we receive something from them to enrich our understanding and our lives. In this way the narratives in African literature instruct not only our understanding of Africa, but also our own self-understanding.

When this kind of reciprocity in understanding becomes possible, then justice across boundaries is made possible. The face of the other is newly visible as my face, and my will to sympathetically understand, to trust, to forgive and to reconcile, all become enhanced. The degree to which my moral and literary imagination can be heightened increases the prospect that there can be justice across boundaries.

NOTES

1. This is a phrase used by Onora O'Neill in her book *Bounds of Justice* (Oxford: Oxford University Press, 2000), chapter 7. Here she wants to avoid what she calls the "messiness" of dealing with older notions like "international justice" or "interstatal justice" or with the current notion of global justice. The first two presuppose that justice is relative to nations or states and is to be extended between nations or states, but, she notes, justice is not simply an item for states, but that it links "substantial political units, businesses, international and governmental agencies, non-government agencies, communities, professional organizations and charities" (115). "On the other hand," she says, "the term 'global justice' seems to beg questions by presupposing that the topic under discussion is a single regime of justice for the world" (115). Thus her term "justice across boundaries."

2. Nussbaum, *Sex and Social Justice*, 161.

3. I have discussed this at greater length in my recent book *Understanding African Philosophy: A Cross-Cultural Approach* (New York: Routledge, 2002), 5–14. The specific reference to *"ubersichtliche" Darstellung* can be found in Wittgenstein's *Philosophical Investigations*, I, paragraph 122.

4. See Philip P. Hallie, *Lest Innocent Blood Be Shed, The Story of the Village of Le Chambon and How Goodness Happened There* (San Francisco: Harper & Row, 1979).

5. One could also say "political boundaries" insofar as at least one Nazi commander, Julius Schmahling, assisted the villagers by turning his eyes away from what the Chambonnais were doing. Cf. *Lest Innocent Blood Be Shed*, 244–247, and in Hallie's book, *In the Eye of the Hurricane: Tales of Good and Evil, Help and Harm* (New York: HarperCollins Publisher, 1997), chapter 5.

We might also see this as an example of the recognition that the Chambonnais felt a "shared responsibility"; they simply could not stand by and "do nothing." There seems to be an intuitive sense of justice in those who have such a capacity for sharing responsibility for harms done. See the interesting study by Larry May, *Sharing Responsibility* (Chicago: University of Chicago Press, 1992), passim.

6. Hallie, *Lest Innocent Blood*, 161.

7. Hallie, *In the Eye of the Hurricane*, 41ff, and larger discussion through page 54.

8. Hallie, *In the Eye of the Hurricane*, chapter 10, "The Hands of Joshua James."

9. Hallie, *In the Eye of the Hurricane*, 172.

10. Hallie, *In the Eye of the Hurricane*, 173.

11. Gaita, *A Common Humanity*, 146.

12. Gaita, *A Common Humanity*, 140f. My emphasis.

13. From Robert Kennedy's memoir, *Thirteen Days: A Memoir of the Cuban Missile Crisis* (1969) as found in Glover, *Humanity*, 213. My emphasis. I do not intend to recount the sequence of the whole crisis—Glover, Robert Kennedy, and others do that well—rather, I will focus on some relevant aspects for our discussion of evoking the moral imagination.

14. Glover, *Humanity*, 219.

15. Glover, *Humanity*, 202.

16. Glover, *Humanity*, 221. An interesting recent account of this crisis is told in retrospect by Kennedy's secretary of defense, Robert McNamara, in the 2004 documentary film *The Fog of War*. This, too, confirms the "moral tone" in the resolution of the crisis.

17. Glover, *Humanity*, 222f.

18. Pumla Gobodo-Mandikizela, *A Human Being Died That Night*, 78.

19. Nussbaum, *Sex and Social Justice*, 170.

20. For a further account of the notion of the "aesthetic consciousness" see my *Understanding African Philosophy: A Cross-Cultural Approach*, 119f.

21. Edward Said, *Culture and Imperialism* (1994), xiii.

22. Appiah, *In My Father's House*, 150. "Realist legitimations of nationalism" are not, of course, all that these novels are.

23. Appiah, *In My Father's House,* 152. My emphasis. Appiah has interesting analyses of several novels of this second stage that show this new narrative concern with suffering and a basic humanism. See his pages 149–157.

24. Johan Snyman, "To Reinscribe Remorse on a Landscape." *Literature and Theology* 13, no. 4 (December 1999): 284f.

25. Sindiwe Magona, *Mother to Mother* (Boston: Beacon Press, 1998). First published by David Philip Publishers, Cape Town, South Africa.

26. Bessie Head, *Tales of Tenderness and Power* (Johannesburg: A.D. Donker, 1989), 141.

27. See her stories "The Lovers," "Village People," and "Property." These stories and more are collected in *Tales of Tenderness and Power.*

28. Bessie Head, *A Woman Alone,* 66.

29. Annie Gagiano, *Achebe, Head, Marechera* (Boulder, CO: Lynne Rienner Publishers, 2000), 160.

30. Gagiano, *Achebe, Head, Marechera,* 160. Gagiano writes at length about the importance of the example of Khama III in *Serowe,* leader of the Sotho people who knew how to exercise a form of "powerless power." Head's understanding of power was that it was potentially embodied in powerlessness that is accompanied by such virtues as a willingness to accommodate and adapt, to shelter and preserve, accompanied by a compassionate dignity. This she believed characterizes southern Africa's most impressive leaders. (See Gagiano, 164–168.)

31. Bessie Head, *A Woman Alone,* 79.

32. Bessie Head, *Tales of Tenderness and Power,* 72.

33. As found in George Pattison, *Kierkegaard: The Aesthetic and the Religious* (London: Macmillan, 1992), 167.

Chapter Five

Justice Across Boundaries II: Human Development and Obligation

The true development of human beings involves much more than mere economic growth. At its heart there must be a sense of empowerment and inner fulfillment. This alone will ensure that human and cultural values remain paramount in a world where political leadership is often synonymous with tyranny and the rule of a narrow elite. *The people's participation in social and political transformation is the central issue of our time.* This can only be achieved through the establishment of societies which place human worth above power, and liberation above control.

[Aung San Suu Kyi*]

In previous chapters we looked at the constitution of our humanity as formed in our relations with others—the meaning of our humanity, in Wittgenstein's words, "is like going up to someone." In the case of the Holocaust, the Nazis found in a Jew and numerous other human beings no "someone" to go up to. The concept of humanity requires mutual recognition of the needs and wants of others and one's self, and the trust needed to mutually fulfill those needs and wants. *Justice, therefore—and especially justice across boundaries (gender, race, nations, cultures, religious traditions)—is a reflection of the kind of reciprocal acknowledgment of the humanness of the other whenever and wherever you "go up to them."*

The issues in justice across boundaries are recognizing, first, the need of the other and then the direction of one's *obligation* to the other if their need is clearly perceived. Balancing off needs with the world's "plenty" is part of what is built into the metaphor of "balancing the scales of social and economic justice" and has been historically identified with "distributive justice." With all the economic and political resources at our human disposal and

81

the circumstances of impoverishment, *"it is hard,"* says Amartya Sen, *"to understand how a compassionate world order can include so many people afflicted by acute misery, persistent hunger and deprived and desperate lives, and why millions of innocent children have to die each year from lack of food or medical attention or social care."*[1]

How can we justly dispose of or distribute the moral, economic, and political resources available to us to meet the challenges of poverty, health, and denial of liberties among so many millions in the world? First there must be a genuine openness to the fact of human differences as well as to the possibility of the reconciliation of those differences. Once again we must remind ourselves of Thoreau's strategy of being present to others, to listen and be responsive. This is not an "empty" exercise but it is an openness to a certain "self-emptying," an abdication of power to render respect and dignity to the other's humanity. Second, on a practical level, social justice across boundaries would be enhanced if the strategy for economic distribution and development were guided by what is called *"the capabilities approach."* The capabilities approach goes beyond what is normally characterized as "third world economic development" strategies to stem the tide of poverty, famine relief, and mass migrations due to civil strife. The capabilities approach has as its goal the liberation of the human self and greater human and social development. In keeping with Seneca: it is development inclusive of a justice that "cultivates humanity." Amartya Sen calls this "development as freedom."

The capabilities approach enables a person to develop certain capacities in their ordinary life; to cultivate intrinsic values and add instrumental value to their life; it creates, as Aung San Suu Kyi said in the beginning of this chapter, "a sense of empowerment and inner fulfillment." The very notion of cultivating intrinsic values in one's life is itself a positive reflection on human capabilities—they can change or develop for better or for worse. The emphasis here is on the positive growth in a person's capabilities. Thus, such capabilities should not be measured by a fixed standard. When Sen calls for a kind of human development "as freedom" his focus is on meeting a person's needs in a way that enables them to transform both their life and their social practices to benefit their community.[2] This is a dynamic process, guided by those "developing," rather than a static process controlled by an external agent/agency for development. This is not to say that external agents or agencies cannot assist with local individual and community development.

The capabilities approach has been most clearly articulated by economist-philosopher Amartya Sen and philosopher Martha Nussbaum. Sen's work earned him the 1998 Nobel Prize in Economics and has made him a major voice in post-colonial studies. Before looking at the capabilities approach as such, however, we need to expose a cultural context where the approach can be applied. We will look at poverty primarily as it has been "catalogued" for us in Sub-Saharan Africa.

POVERTY AND SOCIAL JUSTICE

With the exception of a brief period of prosperity in the 1960s, poverty in Africa has increased sharply in the past four decades due to mass famine, prolonged violence, and economic mismanagement. In the late 1970s Africa had more poverty than Latin America and its relative position to both Latin America and Asia has deteriorated since then. *The inequality between rich and poor in Africa also showed the greatest rise in differential of any continent on the globe.*[3] In spite of this John Iliffe, in his book *The African Poor,* says the mostly rural poor seem to have "lost little of their resilience and capacity for survival."[4] Thus their capability for "freedom" has not been totally destroyed. "The heroism of African history," he continues, "is to be found not in the deeds of kings but in the struggles of ordinary people against the forces of nature and the cruelty of men."[5] This struggle continues even as the odds of hope diminish with AIDS, genocidal and civil wars, and continued political and economic mismanagement. *Having a capacity for survival, however, should not be the goal of a human life.* There is more to our humanity than simple survival.

The strands of suffering and poverty are so interwoven as to be inseparable in Africa. One would be remiss not to detail the role of these two concepts in any ethical discussion of justice and equality. This is done with great skill by Sen. In his book, *Inequality Reexamined*, he challenges John Rawls's notion of "justice as fairness." Sen's counterproposal is more appropriate for considering justice and equality in a cross-cultural and multicultural perspective. In any systematic account of harmdoing and evil, the specific histories of poverty in different cultures and the kinds of poverty should be introduced. One must ask: Is the poverty a consequence of famine, of inaccessibility to food, to larger systemic problems or unemployment, lack of health care, communal "shunning" or "taboos" linked to family structures? Awareness of these heighten one's grasp of the meaning of other ethical concepts such as "care," "compassion," and other "relational" ethical concepts found, for example, at the center of recent communitarian and feminist ethical theory debates.

Suffering and poverty are significant moral concepts, not just descriptive ones. When thinking about justice and equality, for example, in the African context, "suffering" and "poverty" become, in Sen's theoretical scheme, "focal variables—the variable(s) on which the analysis focuses, in comparing different people." With the use of "focal variables" the judgment and measurement of inequality or injustice is seen as "thoroughly dependent on the choice of the variable," for example, income, happiness, wealth, kinds of resources, and needs.[6] One of the benefits of Sen's "focal variables" is that they point out the differences and diversities between peoples and situations. He says "that 'poverty' is a major evaluative concern in most societies, and how we identify poverty is a matter of some practical moment in the contexts compared."[7] For example, what is often measured as "absolute poverty" according to "income level" may not be a good measure of one's happiness or one's sense of empowerment or capacity to maintain a level of dignity in one society compared to another. If one compares poverty as measured by an income "poverty line" or access to "commodities," for example, as is done in the United States,[8] with poverty in Africa by the same standard, you simply multiply your poverty statistics in Africa and do little to understand poverty and its relationship to the kind of suffering experienced in Africa. Nor would you have given consideration to different ways in which moral character is formed, its relationship to community and family structures, or to such notions as *ubuntu*, which in some contexts may be significant for our understanding of mutual patterns of support within communities.[9]

If, however, explicit consideration is given to the relative levels of poverty with respect to kinds of suffering and deprivations in different spaces and how that may limit "the capacity to lead secure and worthwhile lives," then the variable of poverty allows a different reading of the space and people. This would have important effects on choosing development strategies and how best programs of wealth distribution or capital investment should take place. Health care delivery systems, for example, may have more to do with the limiting of poverty and giving people a capacity to lead a secure and worthwhile life than one's level of income. Here we find poverty closely linked with issues of development and the distribution of food and availability of basic services. To see the linkage between poverty and development strategies is, in itself, an important ethical issue that is receiving much current attention.[10]

With respect to what are called "capability factors," the understanding of poverty may vary considerably. For example, the "poverty line" measure in the United States relates in part to a family's capability to purchase certain consumer goods. In an African context having similar consumer goods may be irrelevant (or at least less relevant) to one's happiness and well-being. More important factors would be adequate nourishment and healthcare, the capability to lead a life without shame, and some social freedoms, that is, to move about without coercion or to participate in the decision making of your community. This, of course, may change as over-all consumptive patterns or standards of living change in the society. But the "dignity" associated with "poverty" in Africa asks little—or at least less—of consumptive powers. Rather, a human being expects *to be capable* of certain pleasures or freedoms above adequate nourishment, shelter, and health care. Sen defines poverty as "the lack of freedom to have or to do basic things that you value."[11] "Well-being" itself may be understood differently. So the questions: Whose well-being? Which capabilities? are crucial in evaluating and understanding the moral relevance of poverty. In considering who is poor and why, Sen would have us ask not what minimal commodities or what income level a person may have, *but what capabilities they have to do certain things they value and that show their overall well-being.* David Crocker says of Sen's view: "Capabilities add something intrinsically and not merely instrumentally valuable to a human life, namely positive freedom [or expressive freedom] in the sense of available and worthwhile options."[12]

Understanding the differences in a concept's meaning and use is crucial and seeing connections between "focal variables" and the community's over-all functioning and well-being is essential to establishing patterns of social justice. Sen concludes, "The ordering of poverty and the identification of the poor may be very different if it is done entirely in terms of the size of income (as is the standard practice in most countries) compared with what it would be if the focus is on *capability failure.* . . . By focusing poverty study specifically on incomes as such, crucial aspects of deprivation may be entirely lost."[13] And in a later work he says, "poverty must be seen as the deprivation of basic capabilities rather than merely as lowness of incomes, which is the standard criterion of identification of poverty."[14]

There is poverty virtually everywhere, but the connections of poverty to both family and to the political, economic, and environmental factors of a region make its nature complex and important for any meaningful discussion of ethics or economic justice. On this complexity, moral philosophers like Sen and Nussbaum have shaped a new ethical landscape related to issues of Third World development and justice.[15] We will look at some of the important ideas given us by Sen and Nussbaum with respect to justice across boundaries and with respect to freedoms and equality.

CAPABILITIES AND DEVELOPMENT

So what does all of this have to do with social justice, with how best to enhance development schemes for poorer nations, and with promoting more equitable and just distribution of the world's resources across boundaries? Sen argues that the primary task of development is to do away with the deprivations that constrain a person from the freedom to lead a life she has reason to value. Whether those deprivations are poverty or ill health, or restriction by gender to participate in meaningful decisions concerning her life and the life of her community. This involves, says Sen, a twofold process: (a) "the process of enhancing individual freedoms and (b) the social commitment to help to bring this about."[16] What he refers to as a social commitment is the same as social justice, that is, "for people to be able to take part in the social decisions, if they so choose."[17] The commitment needed to enable new capabilities as freedoms must also come from a sense of responsibility on the part of those of us who are not in a state of deprivation. Sen says: "As people who live—in a broad sense— together, we cannot escape the thought that the terrible occurrences that we see around us are quintessentially our problems. They are our responsibility— whether or not they are also anyone else's. As competent human beings, we cannot shirk the task of judging how things are and what needs to be done. As reflective creatures we have the ability to contemplate the lives of others."[18]

Sen also says "the greatest relevance of ideas of justice lies in the identification of *patent injustice,* on which reasoned agreement is possible, rather than in the derivation of some extant formula for how the world should be precisely run."[19] Here, if we take a closer look at cases of clear injustice, we are more likely to be able to judge what needs doing. He strongly recommends what he calls:

> an approach to justice and development that concentrates on substantive freedoms inescapably focused on the agency and judgment of individuals; they cannot be seen merely as patients to whom benefits will be dispensed by the process of development. Responsible adults must be in charge of their own well-being; it is for them to decide how to use their capabilities. But the capabilities that a person does actually have (and not merely theoretically enjoys) depend on the nature of social arrangements, which can be crucial for individual freedoms. And there the state and society cannot escape responsibility.[20]

Sen clearly wants to separate his capabilities approach from charity! He wants each individual to have a capacity to freely participate in the decisions of his or her community and to have a sense of responsibility for the community to which he or she belongs. This is a paramount feature of a "deliberative democracy" as we shall see in the next chapter.

Sen's capabilities approach in development has a very clear aim—to create "*opportunities to achieve valued outcomes.*"[21] This is a development strategy that clearly has a similar vision in mind that Brien had when he said that justice should "aim for moral outcomes." This is an intrinsic moral approach to justice linked with development; it is not pointing to instrumental ends or ends of individual self-interest as do utilitarian and libertarian development strategies respectively.

Martha Nussbaum, often in collaboration with Sen and in basic agreement with his approach to justice and development, makes very clear what she believes is an essential ingredient for social justice in every society across the globe. She says:

> Social support for basic life functions, including prominently the basic liberties, is what we owe to peoples humanity and dignity. It also makes good social sense, freeing people to be agents in socially productive ways. Every society, then, needs to decide what struggles people should not have to fight for themselves without social support.[22]

Her "list of basic human capacities" *owed* to all (including women) are "support for nutrition, health, shelter, education, and physical safety, and it also owes them effective guarantees of the major liberties of expression, conscience, and political participation."[23]

Nussbaum made the specific point of "including women" because she has traveled the globe and seen how often and how explicitly women are not accorded their due sense of "depth" and dignity. Nussbaum puts her position in the strongest of terms: "There are *universal obligations* to protect human functioning and its dignity, and that the dignity of women is equal to men."[24] The statistics on women's equality worldwide are appalling.[25] This reality leads Nussbaum to opt for the "capabilities approach" to try and assess and improve their quality of life.

Catherine MacKinnon goes further and makes "the Kantian demand that women be treated as ends in themselves, centers of agency and freedom rather than merely as adjuncts to the plans of men."[26] Here, too, we are reminded of Luce Irigaray's demand for autonomy and individual identity of two, man and woman; that they each be given full ontological status—to be, fully, who each is. MacKinnon, Nussbaum, and Irigaray (and others) support legislation to demand such recognition and active treatment. Such laws are not saying that women could not surmount life's obstacles on their own; they frequently have done so. Rather "it is to say that no woman should have to surmount [such obstacles as sexual assault or harassment, for example]; that the dignity of a person demand that she not be treated this way."[27]

It is often argued that different cultural contexts may justify disparities between men and women in equality and quality of life—a kind of cultural relativism. One such relativist tack argues that justice applies primarily to the "public sphere" while much of traditional and/or religious life (with respect to the life of women, for example) takes place in the "private sphere." On this point Onora O'Neill says:

> Relativized accounts of justice . . . nearly [always] relegate (varying portions of) women's lives to a "private" sphere, within which the political virtue of justice has no place, and see state boundaries as limits of justice, appeals to actual traditions [religious or otherwise] tend both to endorse institutions that exclude women from the "public" sphere, where justice is properly an issue, and to insulate one "public" sphere from another.[28]

I believe that our earlier arguments about the structure of *suggnome* or emotional receptivity and seeing oneself in the other, even with all our differences and distances apart, effectively address our commonness (men and women) as human beings; they also speak in support of Nussbaum's justification for common basic capabilities essential to qualities of life and to universal obligations that *all persons* have within their communities and between communities to provide for and enhance those capabilities.

OBLIGATIONS

A central question following our argument to this point is: How do we get humanity to the point of becoming agents for justice—agents for the "universal" implementation of basic capabilities? Or as Simone Weil has similarly asked: How do we become actors who are truly, madly "struggling for justice?" In her more poetic answer to these questions, Simone Weil introduces the concept of the "madness of love." Such "madness of love" is precisely a doggedly applied compassion for those who suffer an injustice wherever and whenever they occur, and its replacement by some sense of beauty and human fulfillment. This madness has an obligatory note to it. She says:

> The madness of love draws one to discern and cherish equally, in all human milieux without exception, in all parts of the globe, the fragile earthly possibilities of beauty, of happiness and of fulfillment; to want to preserve them all with an equally religious care; and where they are absent, to want to rekindle tenderly the smallest traces of those which have existed, the smallest seeds of those which can be born.

What we need is for the spirit of justice to dwell within us. The spirit of justice is nothing other than the supreme and perfect flower of the madness of love.[29]

The work of justice and compassion go hand in hand. As do the work of justice and trust, justice and mercy, justice and development, and justice and reconciliation. These pairings cannot be torn asunder and retain the integrity of a meaningful concept of justice.

There is one last strategy to put before us and this has been clearly articulated by Onora O'Neill in her *Bounds of Justice*. O'Neill says: "if we can establish some principles of justice, and have at least a practical account of the scope of moral concern, then we may be able to start by identifying what is required in order to work towards just institutions."[30] To identify what is required to work toward just institutions we need neither to be bound to a communitarian position that may bind us to one form or another of relativism, nor to a radical cosmopolitan position that may presuppose a certain metaphysical idealism of a global society with no excluding boundaries. It would simply proceed on the assumption of equality of persons and the goodwill of all human beings. O'Neill plots a compromise path. She suggests that in our contemporary world "even if we cannot establish a convincing account of the metaphysical basis of moral standing, we are committed by our own action to thinking that many outsiders count, but that we need not conclude that all boundaries are unjust."[31] We can think of the State boundaries that presently exist, she says, as "porous"—more open to flows of capital and trade and technical influence and culture and movement of people. This, of course, has been and is happening more rapidly in the past few decades. This has also made the world more vulnerable to the corruptions of those who ignore all moral concern and shun all responsibility to the other, while pursuing an amoral (or immoral) dogmatic (political or religious) agenda of their own. O'Neill asks us to think about how we might "justly view state and other boundaries and the distant strangers who live beyond them," and make a transformation toward a more open global community without doing away with boundaries. She says:

One consideration that should guide us in making or working towards such qualitative transformations is a recognition of the reality that we constantly act in ways that commit us to seeing those on the far sides of existing boundaries, distant strangers though they be, *as having moral standing for us. If we do so, then we shall also have reason to treat distant strangers justly.*[32]

Onora O'Neill has a philosophical strategy worth noting for thinking our way into such a view of just concerns in a global context. In a similar vein to

Simone Weil she says we must start by considering *obligations* rather than *rights*, and in so doing we at least begin with a practical task. Obligations, she says, provide a more coherent "starting point for thinking about ethical requirements, including the requirements of justice."[33] Here is how it might work.

[If we begin] with the traditional, Kantian question "What ought I (or we) do?", rather than with the recipients' question "What ought I (or we) get?, we face realities more forthrightly, and pose a question that we *can* address, even if only by beginning the task of constructing institutions. By contrast, those who put rights first and try to claim them in abstraction from institutions will not know where to lodge their claims. The perspective of obligations is simply more directly connected with action.[34]

What ought I (or we) do? This question gets transformed into the practical task "What do I have by way of resources, talents, capabilities, to do? How can I act to aid the distant stranger? How can I contribute to a more humane world? How can I work to open my own community to others? This form of question is a wonderful platform to have for rethinking justice. Its major flaw, however, comes when we realize that "I or we" may have resources and liberties and capabilities that enable us to "think our way to the Kantian starting point, *but* millions of "distant strangers" have neither liberty, nor energy, nor capabilities to even generate the thought about moral concern. It is with this realization that Sen and Nussbaum believe we must press hard for a "capabilities approach" to help determine how to lift people to a basic level of life/freedom so that such a philosophical question might have meaning for them—even if this can only be done for one person, or one poor community, or one drought stricken, war-torn, health plagued nation state at a time. In the end the lifting up of moral concern cannot be a one-way street. The world must position itself to share with each other across porous boundaries; those who exercise compassion must be prepared to listen and receive from the distant stranger as well.

Sen and Nussbaum have clearly brought a new moral language into development theory and tied it squarely to issues of social justice. They have given a human face to economic theory and practices. To measure poverty by considering a person's capacity to exercise certain freedoms, their ability to function as a human being, and to participate in their community's overall well-being gives voice to the poor in ways that "normal" Western economic and development strategies have not done. Add to this O'Neill's and Simone Weil's concern for beginning with obligations to help, and a case will be made that justice is genuinely aiming for moral outcomes. This radically changes the direction of the development discipline to where the patterns of wealth redistribution may be genuinely affected. The very criteria used by IMF and World Bank for loans and the kind of restrictions wealthy nations apply in their foreign aid schemes, for example, have begun to change substantially in recent years. Sen and others have helped give voice to the poor for greater self-determination in ways that earlier Marxist ideological language was often unable to do. In the African context, for example, if family structure, local traditions, and "basic needs" and their effect on human *capabilities* are looked at differently, they become factors in development and redistribution of wealth equations in ways that have been previously ignored. This discovery in itself gives a practical impetus to the development of specific obligations to improve the flourishing and well-being of others. The practical consequence for development strategies that incorporate these "capabilities" concerns, that embrace the distant stranger, and that continue to struggle for justice with "moral outcomes" are best suited to promote true justice.

NOTES

*Aung San Suu Kyi, *Journal of Democracy* 6, no. 2 (1995).

1. Amartya Sen, *Development As Freedom* (Oxford: Oxford University Press, 1999), 282. My emphasis.

2. This is characterized as an "expressive freedom" (a form of pragmatism) by Jeffrey Stout in his *Democracy and Tradition* (Princeton: Princeton University Press, 2004) as he applies this to how a citizen can more actively participate in the political process of his or her community and thus also take some responsibility for it. See Stout, 80–85.

3. See comparative figures in John Iliffe, *The African Poor* (Cambridge: Cambridge University Press, 1989), 231, and throughout his chapter "The Growth of Poverty in Independent Africa," 230–259. These figures are also spelled out in some detail in Sen, *Development As Freedom,* see chapters 3 and 4.

4. Iliffe, *The African Poor,* 230.

5. Iliffe, *The African Poor,* 1. Desmond Tutu has expressed this same sentiment a number of times, referring to the resilience and dignity of the victims of apartheid evident throughout the hearings of the TRC.

6. Amartya Sen, *Inequality Reexamined* (Cambridge: Harvard University Press, 1995), 2. See also Sen, "Capability and Well-Being," in *The Quality of Life*, ed. Martha Nussbaum and Sen (New York: Oxford University Press, 1993), and David Crocker, "Functioning and Capability: The Foundations of Sen's and Nussbaum's Development Ethic," *Political Theory* 20, no. 4 (November 1992): 595f.

7. Sen, *Inequality Reexamined,* 107.

8. An article in *The New York Times,* "How to Define Poverty? Let Us Count the Ways," by Louis Uchitelle, Saturday, May 26, 2001, shows how the U.S. government has used a fixed income level to measure poverty since the mid-1960s. This is far behind the current discussions and thinking among development ethicists, social policy makers, and even the World Bank.

9. In our next chapter we will explore the meaning and use of such concepts as an individual's relationship to community and *ubuntu* (a connectedness producing love, forgiveness, generosity) as these are given new life through some African philosophers and through the TRC process.

10. There is a growing "new discipline" called "international development ethics," that is interdisciplinary rather than the preserve of just philosophers. Sen's and Martha Nussbaum's works have been vital to the formation of this new discipline. A wider consensus on development policy as it relates to issues like hunger and poverty is sought from both "insiders" and "outsiders" concerned with any new development strategies. Also central to international development ethics are issues concerning the overall well-being of people in ways that Sen has suggested. David A. Crocker says, for example, that "Nutritional well-being is only one element in human well-being; the overcoming of transitory or chronic hunger also enables people and their governments to protect and promote other ingredients of well-being. Being adequately nourished, for instance, contributes to healthy functioning that is both good in itself and indispensable to the ability to avoid premature death and fight off or recover from disease. Having nutritional well-being and good health, in turn, is crucial to acquiring and exercising other valuable capabilities such as being able to learn, think, deliberate, and choose as well as to be a good pupil, friend, householder, parent, worker, or citizen." Crocker, "Hunger, Capability, and Development," in *World Hunger and Morality* ed. Aiken and La Follette (Upper Saddle River, NJ: Prentice Hall, 1996). For a foundational essay in development ethics see David A. Crocker, "Toward Development Ethics," *World Development*, 19, no. 5 (1991): 457–483.

11. As found in Uchitelle, *The New York Times*, May 26, 2001.

12. David A. Crocker, "Functioning and Capability: The Foundations of Sen's and Nussbaum's Development Ethic, Part 2," in *Women, Culture, and Development: A Study of Human Capabilities* ed. Martha Nussbaum and Jonathan Glover (Oxford: Clarendon Press, 1995), 159.

13. Sen, *Inequality Reexamined*, 112f. My emphasis. See also Crocker, "Hunger," 611. For other relevant philosophical literature on international development ethics related to justice and building "civic society," see David A. Crocker and Toby Linden, eds., *Ethics of Consumption: The Good Life, Justice and Global Stewardship* (Lanham, MD, New York and London: Rowman & Littlefield, 1998), and essays in Nussbaum and Sen, eds., *The Quality of Life* (New York: Oxford University Press, 1993).

14. Sen, *Development as Freedom*, 87.

15. See Nussbaum and Sen, eds., *The Quality of Life*. A summary of their respective views can be found in David A. Crocker, "Functioning and Capability: The Foundations of Sen's and Nussbaum's Development Ethic," *Political Theory* 20, no. 4. (November 1992): 584–612. Also Nussbaum discusses numerous examples from women's lives in the African context in her *Sex and Social Justice* (Oxford: Oxford University Press, 1999). See especially chapter 1, "Women and Cultural Universals," 29–54.

16. Sen, *Development as Freedom*, 298.

17. Sen, *Development as Freedom*, 242.

18. Sen, *Development as Freedom*, 282f.

19. Sen, *Development as Freedom*, 287.
20. Sen, *Development as Freedom*, 288.
21. Sen, *Development as Freedom*, 291.
22. Nussbaum, *Sex and Social Justice,* 20.
23. Nussbaum, *Sex and Social Justice,* 20.
24. Nussbaum, *Sex and Social Justice,* 30. My emphasis.
25. Nussbaum, *Sex and Social Justice,* see 31f, for figures.
26. Nussbaum, *Sex and Social Justice,* 20.
27. Nussbaum, *Sex and Social Justice,* 20
28. Onora O'Neill, *Bounds of Justice*, 143.
29. Simone Weil, "Are We Struggling for Justice?", 9.
30. Onora O'Neill, *Bounds of Justice,* 199.
31. O'Neill, *Bounds of Justice*, 201.
32. O'Neill, *Bounds of Justice*, 201f. My emphasis.
33. O'Neill, *Bounds of Justice,* 199.
34. O'Neill, *Bounds of Justice*, 199.

Chapter Six

Restorative Justice
and Democratic Deliberation

Democracy in its present Western form arouses skepticism and distrust in many parts of the world. . . . The reason for this distrust does not, I think, lie in some kind of fundamental opposition in most of the world to democracy as such and to the values it has made possible. It lies in something else: the limited ability of today's democratic world to step beyond its own shadow, or, rather, the limits of its own present spiritual and intellectual condition and direction, and thus its limited ability to address humanity in a genuinely universal way.

[Vaclav Havel, from a speech upon reception of the Indira Gandhi Prize,
New Delhi, February 8, 1994]

We can live more sensibly with one another if we try. For example, there are differences in both attitude and disposition that go with the concepts of justice understood from a *retributive perspective* and *a restorative perspective.* We have often used the noun forms "retributive justice" and "restorative justice" as if these were self-contained, competing "theories of justice." This leads a reader to think these are two distinctive *kinds* of legal or judicial systems, each with different approaches to thinking about punishment, equity, and mercy or forgiveness. Although there is some truth in making this distinction in this way, we need to begin thinking differently about the concept of "justice" itself and how aspects of current legal systems might be altered to embrace a more restorative perspective. We need, as Vaclav Havel says, "to step beyond our own shadow." I believe that the concept "restorative justice" should be understood as part of what justice means in a truly "enlightened" and humane society; that the restorative perspective should be embraced in thinking about forms of punishment, equity, and mercy or forgiveness in consideration of a wide variety of criminal and civil wrongs done to

95

human beings. The very notion of "balancing the scales" can be achieved in a number of creative ways that have more lasting and peaceful consequences on the civil order of society than is reflected in most "retributive" oriented legal systems in place around the globe. A more restorative perspective could renew trust in the "spiritual" direction of justice in democratic societies. Following is a broader look at the character and virtues of justice from a restorative perspective.

RESTORATIVE JUSTICE

Let us start by contrasting an aspect of the two notions of a "retributive" attitude and a "restorative" attitude with respect to justice. The contrast is between retaliation for a wrong done versus forgiveness or reconciliation for a wrong done. Jonathan Sacks in his book *The Dignity of Difference* writes the following:

> Retaliation is the instinctual response to perceived wrong. Montesquieu wrote that "every religion which is persecuted becomes itself persecuting; for as soon as by some accidental turn it arises from persecution, it attacks the religion which persecuted it." Nationalism, said Isaiah Berlin, "is usually the product of a wound inflicted by one nation on the pride or territory of another." Historic grievances are rarely forgotten. They become part of a people's collective memory, the narrative parents tell their children, the story from which a group draws its sense of identity. A note of injustice not yet avenged is written into the script that is then re-enacted at moments of crisis.

He then adds that the intervention of the restorative attitude of forgiveness can alter the retributive cycle.

> In a world without forgiveness, evil begets evil, harm generates harm, and there is no way short of exhaustion or forgetfulness of breaking the sequence. Forgiveness breaks the chain. It introduces into the logic of interpersonal encounter the unpredictability of grace. . . . Forgiveness means that we are not destined endlessly to replay the grievances of yesterday. It is the ability to live with the past without being held captive by the past. It would not be an exaggeration to say that forgiveness is the most compelling testimony to human freedom. It is about the action that is not reaction.[1]

Human rights advocate Michael Ignatieff in his book *The Warrior's Honor* (1997) wrote the following about revenge or the embedded nature of the retributive attitude:

The chief moral obstacle in the path of reconciliation is the desire for revenge. Now, revenge is commonly regarded as a low and unworthy emotion, and because it is regarded as such, its deep moral hold on people is rarely understood. But revenge—morally considered—is a desire to keep faith with the dead, to honor their memory by taking up their cause where they left off. Revenge keeps faith between generations; the violence it engenders is a ritual form of respect for the community's dead—therein lies its legitimacy. Reconciliation is difficult precisely because it must compete with the powerful alternative morality of violence. Political terror is tenacious because it is an ethical practice. It is a cult of the dead, a dire and absolute expression of respect.[2]

Jonathan Sacks then reflects on Ignatieff's clear and haunting account of revenge and tries to offer a response to it. Sacks wants to show that when we tie forgiveness to justice there is a possible way out of the cycle of revenge or at least some way to counter the "ethical practice" and "cultic" nature of revenge. He says, "Justice takes the sense of wrong and transforms it from personal retaliation—revenge—to the impersonal process of law—retribution. Forgiveness is the further acknowledgment that justice alone may not be enough to silence the feelings of the afflicted. . . . Justice rights wrongs; forgiveness rebuilds broken relationships."[3]

Sacks wants to go further, however. He wants to show that "justice and forgiveness go hand-in-hand." I think, however, an even better way to think about justice and forgiveness is in the manner that we discussed justice and mercy in Chapter 3. Forgiveness, like mercy, must be infused into, be part and parcel of the very concept of justice. Not that one always forgives, nor that forgiveness must always be a consideration when justice is served. However, forgiveness should be able to come-to-the-fore—come to mind—when justice considers the toughest violations of human rights and worst kinds of human violence, or at such moments in political transformations where there is an imperative to "rebuild broken relationships." This has been a prime consideration in the many cases where "Truth Commissions" have been under consideration in countries making a transition from oppressive totalitarian regimes to one or another form of democracy. As we have seen, this seemed to be part of what was required of "justice" during the South African TRC and in the overall process of national healing.[4]

An altogether different way of approaching justice is by *not* thinking of it as a mechanism designed to "get one's due" or balancing the scales by seeking retribution for wrongs—the "just deserts" approach. Rather by thinking of justice primarily as a process through which order and harmony are "restored" to society and a sense of civic balance is retained. This latter approach is called "restorative justice" and is rooted in numerous forms of traditional consensus or communalists' models of justice. This is a more *deliberative model* with the aim of reconciling victims and perpetrators of crimes with one another to achieve a more cooperative and less violent society. The world was startled and challenged when Nelson Mandela and other South African leaders from all racial communities, after the fall of apartheid, called for reconciliation rather than revenge against the former apartheid regime. South Africa advanced a plan both through its new constitution and its TRC that enabled it to move quickly toward a more democratic and peaceful multi-racial society—a society that believed that the truth of its past, if fully revealed, could lead to forgiveness and healing between former enemies, and prove to be a powerful instrument for justice in a new South Africa.

Since its transformation to a majority democracy in South Africa there has been a number of legislative moves toward a more restorative perspective on justice in some areas. For example, in 2001, "white South Africans embraced a new youth justice bill that in its preamble set the indigenous restorative notion of *ubuntu*—the idea that our humanity is relationally tied to the humanity of those we live with—as the fundamental objective of the legislation. *Ubuntu* is the notion that enabled Mandela to construe even the supporters of apartheid as inextricably its victims."[5]

Let me say more here about the kind of justice that many believe was achieved through the TRC process. Wilhelm Verwoerd articulates two clear achievements of the TRC. First he says: "the relationships between amnesty, justice and the TRC can be seen as one of 'partial justice' rather than 'no justice.' Instead of regarding amnesty and the TRC process simply as a 'sacrifice' of individual justice, we may describe the TRC process as a 'principled compromise' that sacrifices some, but retains other, key elements of justice." The elements of justice retained are linked with the idea of a "restorative justice."[6]

Second Verwoerd says: "From the perspective of 'restorative justice,' the TRC is not a 'second-best option' but a contribution to a different, more complete kind of justice."[7] On this point we can link justice with such notions as forgiveness, self-esteem, compassion, and mercy, and with ideas of equity and obligations found in Nussbaum, O'Neill, and Simone Weil.

It may not be self-evident to everyone that a community, compassion-based justice system—justice from a more restorative perspective—is better than an individual, rights-based justice system—a more retributive, "just desserts" perspective. But if one wants a system of justice that "aims for moral outcomes," as Brien says, or as Seneca suggests a legal system that "cultivates humanity" and moves away from cruelty or retributive anger [revenge], then there is every reason to include mercy and forgiveness, and move toward a more compassion-based, restorative justice perspective. There is surely a case to be made for the greater value in "restoring" a community, compassion-based justice when a society has been fractured and great harm done to its people, and when there is some evidence that traditions in the local society suggest communal-based democratic structures even if they have been badly bruised or fragmented. In such cases there is more likely to be a prospect for civic cohesion and greater openness to reconciliation.

In the South African situation—and indeed in most human societies—it seems both plausible and preferable to opt for a "restorative" rather than a "retributive" kind of justice. This was "the best option" given the political realities of South Africa's peaceful, negotiated transition and the open and transparent process of its Commission on Truth and Reconciliation. Likewise, other democratic societies—especially those societies that are multicultural or pluralistic in nature—could benefit from a more compassion-based, restorative justice perspective. In societies where differences must be respected and in which there is a continual need for reconciliation, a compassion-based perspective on justice would best serve the end of greater justice, in it broadest sense, for all.

There are numerous current examples of communities and even nations adopting restorative models of justice because of their inherent deliberative democratic procedures. Their appeal is that they tend to be less punitive justice systems, and systems that place a strong emphasis on consent of the governed and on victim empowerment. Furthermore, *a restorative model reestablishes justice as the moral and social virtue it should be*. A leading philosopher-theorist of restorative justice, John Braithwaite of Australia, writes the following: "Restorative justice can deliver freedom as non-domination in a way just deserts cannot, and citizens in democracies have profoundly deep aspirations to freedom and deep distrust of domination."[8] New laws like the Patriot Act in the United States legal system only serve to deepen distrust of domination and increase the perception of others that our aspirations for freedom and justice are shallow at best. Such a conception of justice as the Patriot Act suggests is no virtue! Following a Chorus line in *Antigone*, I ask: "what have we learned about justice?" Is it a legal concept and tied simply to the rule of law? Or is justice a leading moral virtue in societies? How are we to think about justice?

What are some of the implications in moving toward a sense of justice that is restorative rather than retributive at every level in a society's life? Such a move is thought by many to be totally unrealistic. I am convinced, however, by reading of acts of mercy and compassion through the TRC process, and through many years of research and writing on the twentieth-century French political philosopher Simone Weil and her revisions of justice around the concepts of "attention" and "compassion," that a different and more "reconciliatory" way of thinking about justice is possible and realistic. I am also encouraged by the increasing examples where *the practice* of forms of restorative justice are, in fact, taking hold in promising ways. Braithwaite's recent work evaluates the growing number of cases of restorative justice around the globe.[9]

The restorative perspective in justice is not a radically new idea. However, it stands in radical contrast with the retributive patterns of justice established in Western societies following the Enlightenment. A restorative perspective on justice challenges our imagination in all civic contexts but especially in those emerging from conditions of excessive violence. The twentieth century has cast a great cloud of violence on the horizon of this present century. In previous chapters we have noted the global dis-equilibrium of great wealth and great poverty that promote a variety of forms of violence and inequality. We seem hopelessly mired in this disparity and only "tinker" with present economic and social justice systems to try to find a way forward. How can a restorative perspective on justice help us?

Braithwaite notes this remark of an Irish Republican Army ex-prisoner made at a recent conference in Northern Ireland: "Restorative justice is not just about crime, it is about peace and a way of bringing up our children that is less punitive and more decent. It is a holistic philosophy."[10] Restorative justice calls for a change in how we live our life. In retributive justice systems, civil and criminal litigation is more preoccupied, says Braithwaite, with deciding "whether litigants should give their adversaries what they deserve [than] whether they should concentrate on fixing the problem."[11] Restorative justice is more about how we can integrate, or better "ingrain" certain values into our civic life than it is about a competing "theory of justice." Braithwaite says that restorative justice programs should be evaluated by how effectively they deliver restorative values. These values—most of which we have already identified with a classical concept of justice—are basically those found in the numerous international human rights agreements such as restoration of human dignity, restoration of property loss, restoration of communities and environments, freedom, peace, and self-determination. Restorative justice is also designed to encourage such values as trust, mercy in legal justice, reflective attention or mindfulness to others, and compassion.[12]

A truly astonishing thing about these values is that they are being worked on very diligently in many communities and nations throughout the globe. The institution of restorative justice can be found to be working in New Zealand Maori and North American Indian communities, in South Africa, in the restoration of peace in some war-torn nations such as Bosnia-Herzegovina, Mozambique and Namibia, in the New Zealand and Australian legal systems, in *Bang jiao* teams in China, and anti-bullying and whole school programs in many local communities in the west—to mention but a few.

Restorative values were also central in selected reparations to wronged communities, for example, in the Japanese-American internment during World War II, the "Mabo" aboriginal case in Australia and reparations for the survivors of the "stolen generation" in Tasmania as discussed in Chapter 2, and the Canadian aboriginal people's land claims leading to a new aboriginal province. The idea of reparations as part of a restorative process has also been a part of a number of recent truth commissions, for example in Argentina, Chile, Germany, and South Africa.[13] Braithwaite concludes from these and many more examples that "there does seem to be empirical grounds for optimism that restorative justice can 'work' in restoring victims, offenders, and communities . . . [and] that restorative justice mostly works well in granting justice, closure, restoration of dignity, transcendence of shame, and healing for victims."[14] This is so primarily because restorative justice involves the wrongdoers in taking responsibility for the consequences of their crimes. As Braithwaite says: "Restorative justice is about nurturing the taking of active responsibility, especially by offenders who are given the most compelling reasons to do so by the discussion of the consequences of a crime. *A wrongdoer taking responsibility is a morally superior outcome than being made to be responsible by an imposed sanction.*"[15]

It is also a promising fact that restorative justice is effective in crossing boundaries especially as it concerns NGOs in conflict resolution, interethnic disputes, and some minor territorial disputes. In these, adopting a more reflective, deliberative process has proven effective in surfacing shared values regarding common land use, environmental issues, and in agreeing on common needs that all humans should have available to them. As Braithwaite says: "Restorative justice should settle for the procedural requirement that the parties talk until they feel that peace has been restored on the basis of a discussion of all the injustices they see as relevant to the case."[16] One outcome of cross-boundary deliberation is a freedom from domination by one side of the dispute over another. This freedom as nondomination is a desired outcome of a restorative perspective. It remains part of our *Realpolitik* political arrangements that "dominating powers always act in the interest of further domination,"[17] and the retributive perspective does little to neutralize this idea. Thus, Braithwaite concludes: "Justice is that set of arrangements [arrived at by deliberation] that allow people to make claims against another individual and institutions in order to secure freedom against the possibility of domination."[18] It seems clear, for example, that the preemptive actions taken by the American and British coalition in Iraq has had domination as a primary goal and thus has actually minimized freedom—at least for a longer time than anticipated—for the Iraqi people.[19]

Now what are some of the more theoretical arguments given in support of restorative justice, and how can they help us think about dealing with communities that are moving from past atrocities or gross injustices to a more democratic and cooperative partnership?

First, as seen through the South African TRC process, there was greater equity between perpetrators of crimes and victims. This is often referred to as "equality of justice," where the perpetrators were asked (or coerced into) taking responsibility for the consequences of their crimes. It allowed victims to determine what forms of restoration are more important to them and accorded victims a greater level of care. In more retributive systems, the resulting proportional punishments for criminals has been nicely characterized by Martin Wright as follows: "Balancing the harm done *by* the offender with further harm inflicted *on* the offender only adds to the total amount of harm in the world."[20]

The restorative process alternative to "inflicting further harm" has been summarized nicely by South African research student Debra Dalton. Ms. Dalton writes:

> The process of restorative justice is the bringing of victims, perpetrators and bystanders into dialogue, "to discuss how they have been affected by the harm and come to some agreement as to what would be done to right any wrongs suffered."[21] The reciprocity required of participants by the restorative justice process is an important aspect of justice. Reciprocity, philosophers Amy Gutmann and Dennis Thompson argue, is democracy in practice: "A reciprocal perspective is one that cannot be reasonably rejected by any citizen committed to democracy because it requires only that each person seeks terms of cooperation that respect all as free and equal citizens."[22] The participatory process emphasizes the need to respect each other's humanity and dignity—a need deeply felt by members of once divided societies like South Africa during apartheid.[23]

Another major aim of restorative justice is to attain *freedom from domination* and *empowerment* for all parties in a dispute, especially victims. This allows parties to express their grievances and claims, and avoid domination from a third party's decisions. The question: "Whose justice?" is relevant here—The courts? The prosecutors? The victims? To reasonably/deliberatively answer this question better enables *a moral outcome* in disputes.

Greater equity in disputes and more deliberation will help avoid wrongful punishment. The State of Illinois in the United States has recently been forced into re-examining its death penalty law—a hallmark of many retributive systems—because since 1997 when they established capital punishment, thirteen death row prisoners have been exonerated while eight have been executed. In a rush to "react" to terrible crimes and punish proportionally, this equal reaction produced grossly unequal results—and thirteen innocent people could have been executed. How do you implement a death penalty fairly and not risk innocent lives? And on another front, the spiral of retribution and violence in the Middle East has done nothing but compound the "total amount of harm in the world." To paraphrase Hannah Arendt, to practice violence only leads to a more violent world.

Most important, however, in the practice of restorative justice according to Braithwaite, as was noted earlier in this chapter, is to nurture "taking active responsibility for righting the wrong, . . . especially by offenders who are given the most compelling reasons to do so by the discussion of the consequences of a crime. A wrongdoer *taking responsibility* is a morally superior outcome than *being made to be responsible* by an imposed sanction."[24] The South African TRC amnesty hearings where victims' families participated and supported amnesty-as-mercy produced some astonishing "restorative results." In the spirit of exercising our moral imaginations again, I will note briefly two cases from the TRC. The first example, referred to earlier, is seen in the amnesty results of the killers of American Fulbright scholar, Amy Biehl, and the active participation in the hearings of Amy Biehl's mother and father.

The Biehls, to honor their daughter, wanted to contribute to the aim of reconciliation of the commission's work for South African society. They acted directly to affect the young killers, and the transformation in the lives of these young men has been remarkable.[25] In discussing this episode, Wilhelm Verwoerd concludes:

During the amnesty hearings Pieter and Linda Biehl made it clear that for them punishment should be subordinated to the primary goal of reconciliation. A closer look reveals that the gradual building of relationships of trust extended to include the Biehl family and some of the perpetrator's families. Re-integration of the successful amnesty applicants into their community is also a central theme. At the amnesty hearing Ntobeko Penni [the attacker who struck the fatal blow] "apologized" by merely expressing regret that they killed someone who could have been useful in their struggle, but as the relationship with the Biehls grew he became more and more interested in who Amy Biehl really was, named their social club after her, and became actively involved in organizing the annual commemoration of Amy's death. I would interpret these actions as the acceptance of responsibility for restitution. Throughout the Biehls played a central role in working out, together with perpetrators and their families, a healing response to a terrible tragedy. Thus, in this case, the amnesty process can be said not only to have promoted reconciliation, but also to have contributed to the rendering of justice, restorative justice.[26]

A second compelling example is found in an affidavit given before the TRC amnesty committee submitted by Nelson Papiyana. He describes the tragic killing of his beloved son in a drive-by shooting, by two supporters of the "Afrikaner Weerstandsbeweging" (a rightwing paramilitary organization):

The deceased Vuyani Kenneth Papiyana was at the time of the incident, a 26-year old student at [a] teachers' college. We were very proud of Vuyani, he set a fine example for the other children, did very well at school and we had no doubt that he would one day become an excellent teacher. On this particular day, he was home for the short holiday following the closure of universities and technicons during the period of election.

On the day in question I was with Vuyani and Madoda there at about 14h00. They had come to vote, but due to the fact that the queues were too long, decided to go to another polling station. . .

After 21h00 that night, I was called to the telephone. It was the police, who notified me of my son's death. I immediately went to my house where I informed my wife. We were devastated.

My wife told me that . . . at about 20h00 that evening, Vuyani and Madoda requested her permission to have the vehicle because they wanted to visit their friend in Mahlakeng near Randfontein. They were excited and happy, like most people in South Africa.

That day that we had been looking forward to for decades — the day that symbolized freedom for all of us — had finally arrived. 27 April 1994 was the birth of a new democracy in our beloved country, but to me, it also meant the death of our beloved son. I was a father without a child.

During the trial one of the killers requested a meeting with Mr. Papiyana. "I spoke to my wife and she said that she would not be able to face the murderer of her son. I decided that I wanted to see this man and I would listen to what he had to say and then form an opinion about the situation." . . .

On 3 October 1994 I met with Mr. Pyper and his wife in [my legal representative's] office. When Mr. Pyper and his wife entered the office I immediately knew that it was the best thing I could ever have done — to see the man who murdered my son face to face. This meeting helped me to overcome some of the emotional problems.

I will never forget the faces of Mr. Pyper and his wife. I could see that Mr. Pyper tried his best to keep his emotions under control. We went into an empty office and Mr. Pyper closed the door behind him. Mrs. Pyper sobbed so much that she could not speak properly. I knew this man was indeed sorry for what he had done and when I offered my hand, he could not grab it quickly enough with both his hands. Tears were running freely down his face.

Mr. Pyper offered me a cheque to the amount of R5200.00 in respect of the funeral costs I incurred. I refused to accept it, but he insisted and I could see that it would ease his pain a bit should I accept it. I could see that after I had talked to Mr. Pyper and his wife and accepted the cheque, that he felt a lot better.

Before this meeting, I thought I would never have the ability to forgive my son's murderers for what they did. In my wildest dreams I never thought this meeting would end with a situation where I was the one comforting my son's murderer and wife. I still wonder a lot what happened to his wife and children.[27]

It is clear that the sheer humanity of people can inspire responsibility. Also at the heart of both of these episodes is a reconciling justice that embraces forgiveness. Jonathan Sacks remarks: "Forgiveness means that we are not destined endlessly to replay the grievances of yesterday. It is the ability to live with the past without being held captive to the past. It would not be an exaggeration to say that forgiveness is the most compelling testimony of human freedom. It is about the action that is not reaction."[28]

DELIBERATIVE DEMOCRACY AND JUSTICE

We will, finally, say a few things about the importance of the *deliberative process* that is at the heart of restorative justice and a democratic civil order. It is also essential to the retrieval of the concept of justice that is at the center of this book. Seldom is it noted in Western political philosophy that a distinction needs to be sharpened between the idea of deliberative democracy and the more familiar idea of a majority rule democracy. There is, however, a substantial global literature on democracy in this deliberative sense. We have already made a strong case that the deliberative democracy central to restorative justice can serve as a corrective to some negative features of majority rule democracy. But again, what is the major fault in majority rule democracy? K. Pranis clearly notes:

If your position has the larger numbers, there is little incentive to seek common ground or ways that the interests of all might be served. In fact, if you can outvote the other position you don't even need to understand that position. Majority rule decision-making often leaves a significant number of people feeling left out, alienated, and resentful because no attempt was made to understand their needs.[29]

By contrast there is inherent value in the conversations, disputations, and reciprocity found in more deliberative democratic processes like town hall meetings, community palavers, and the direct dialogue between victims and perpetrators that go into consensual decision making and in resolving conflicts. There is substantial concurrence among philosophers and political theorists that "[d]isputing over daily injustices is where we learn to become democratic citizens."[30] These are essentially more "democratic processes"—more expressive of the will of the people—than are found in processes that accompany majoritarian democracies.

There are growing debates throughout the globe on how to provide an environment whereby each person may have a stake in the society's decisions and be assured of maintaining their self-respect. Such debates have occurred on the floor of the European Union Parliament, in its bureaucracy in Brussels and in individual E.U. nations; they have occurred in a number of African nations searching for the right democratic balance in making a transition from autocratic or totalitarian rule to forms of modern democracy; and in the United States where majority rule policy, or the control of policies by moneyed interests, seem to drive our political order. In each of these contexts there has been alienation of sometimes a "more than" minority of the society and the disenfranchisement of the voices of many. In these debates what is sought is a democratic environment that displays greater reciprocity between majority and minority interests on a wide range of issues. Let us take a look at a few examples: first, some views of several contemporary African philosophers, then conclude with an interesting position argued by American constitutional and legal theorist Ronald Dworkin.

Ghanaian philosopher Kwasi Wiredu has written several important articles on the idea of what he calls "consensus democracy." He contrasts this "democracy by consensus" with "democracy by the majority rule principle." His intentions are twofold in these essays: first to show "the gross blemishes of majoritarian democracy that in post-colonial Africa have been so utterly crippling in their effects";[31] and second, to encourage a more deliberative process he finds in much African communalism that encourage different "habits of mind." These different "habits of mind" are part of the consensual-deliberative process in his consensus democracy model. *These habits are "belief in dialogue, respect for others, freedom from overweening ambition for power, and openness to mutual accommodations."*[32] These habits are all central elements toward our "thick" revision of justice.

Wiredu argues that majoritarian democracy was imposed upon most African colonies by Western colonial pressures. The Western majoritarian model encourages democracy under a multiparty structure and has within Africa, not surprisingly, led to "frustrations and disaffections," leaving minority parties "outside the corridors of power." This has only exacerbated ethnic rivalries, as "parties" in most African "multiparty" systems have tended to fall along ethnic lines to serve local interests. The elected, majority party, however, makes all the rules to serve its interests. This Wiredu sees as "the most persistent cause of political instability in Africa."[33] In another essay Wiredu writes:

Quite apart from the moral excellence of consensus as an ideal, the need for it is a life-and-death matter in Africa. In the post-colonial period our experiments in democracy have been imitations of Western multi-party majoritarianism. But this has politicized and exacerbated pre-existing dissensions and created new ones with deadly consequences. . . . Frequently, small ethnic groups have been politically marginalized in the face of the dominance of larger ones.[34]

A somewhat different version of this thesis of governance by consensus is developed by political philosopher Mahmood Mamdani of Uganda in his book *Citizen and Subject.* What Mamdani calls the "decentralized despotism" imposed by late colonial rule in Africa he also sees as a primary cause of ethnic rivalry in contemporary social and political life. The legacy of decentralized despotism, furthermore, is *not* a natural evolution of traditional communal or consensual governance patterns in Africa but is a construct of colonialism in order to control the "native problem." Mamdani, like Wiredu, sees this as responsible for much of the instability in Africa. Mamdani makes a very strong case for how the colonials worked hard, using long years of experience in India and in colonies farther to the north in Africa, to undermine the deliberative democratic process in southern Africa and establish a controlled retributive system. They did so in order to assert both local and national despotic control over the rural native peoples—a divide and conquer strategy.[35] It was a process that allowed little or no meaningful local deliberation.

A consensual democracy, according to Wiredu, is a much more representative and deliberative form of government that necessarily must keep the interests of all the members of the society in mind. He says that the consensual model was a premeditated form of governance, and is actually widespread in traditional African society as well as outside Africa—he cites Switzerland and Belgium. He gives many examples from his own Ashanti community. Wiredu says of the Ashanti view that "it was a democracy because government was by the consent, and subject to the control of the people as expressed through their representatives. It was consensual because, as a rule, that consent was negotiated on the principle of consensus following extensive conversation and consultation. (By contrast, the majoritarian system might be said to be, in principle, based on 'consent' without 'consensus'). . . . For all concerned, the [consensual] system was set up for participation in power, not its appropriation, and the underlying philosophy was one of cooperation, not confrontation."[36]

What consensus should do is produce compromises that are acceptable to all, or at least not loathsome to any. What these "deliberative democracy" models show is how people come together to resolve community and personal disputes pertaining to civic order and matters of injustice, and they contribute to community well-being. This empowers ordinary people to be good citizens and to recognize their worth. The very idea of a deliberative democracy is not a natural process. One must be educated into it and given a voice that will be listened to and respected—one must develop what Wiredu has called proper "habits of mind."

Kwame Gyekye, also of Ghana, cites an Akan proverb that says: "Wisdom is not in the head of one person." It is certainly not obvious that when one speaks of "democratic" roots being found in village governance and symbolized by the village palaver, that this closely resembles what is called liberal democratic institutions in the West. It is, however, not a long stretch to discuss the nearness and overlapping values of each. Gyekye goes on to discuss "democratic features of the indigenous system of government," and suggests an ethos for the development of a more modern democratic form of governance. Gyekye says simply: *a democracy is government of, by, and for the people*, and in Africa that means involvement of and by all the people in the decision-making process concerning their general welfare.

A feature of this involvement is the extent to which the people participate at the level of village life through palavers or as represented in village councils. Gyekye cites Ndabaningi Sithole as saying: "Those who have lived in Africa know that the African people are democratic to the point of inaction. Things are never settled until everyone has had something to say. [The traditional African] council allows the free expression of all shades of opinion."[37]

This simplified response does not necessarily make the practice of such a palaver either "democratic" or "philosophical." It does, however, suggest that beyond "a point of inaction" some due process may be taking place and extensive consideration is given to the important issues concerning village life—issues such as fairness, equality, kinds of punishment, general welfare, and the just resolution of disputes. These are, of course, the very issues of concern one will find in nearly all of the recent studies of justice in Western philosophy, for example, in Rawls, Nozick, Dworkin, Sandel, and others. To say this does not make the village process philosophical. However, if one were to look at the individual issues taken up by a village council or sifted through a village palaver, those issues could be used by philosophers in ways that would lead to the gradual development of better governance.

Let us go directly to the specific case of the village palaver and the work of Ernest Wamba Dia Wamba of the Democratic Republic of Congo (DRC) on the meaning of the village palaver for understanding traditional democracy from the central and eastern provinces of the former Congo. Wamba-dia-Wamba, with whom I have had a number of extended conversations on this issue, has observed, "the palaver is an appropriate community method and practice to resolve contradictions among the people and to strengthen organic mutual links of solidarity among all the members of the community."[38] The palaver is a means of "free" or "liberated" speaking by community members, but it is not uncritical or unreflective. If, for example, the equilibrium of a community is threatened, its causes may be identified and dealt with by calling a palaver. This becomes a forum for self-questioning of and by all the community members and it is rule governed "in a manner sanctioned by the ancestors."[39] Furthermore, there are usually leaders, the *Nzonzi*, who are known specialists or who emerge on the spot, as "masters of the clarification of speech." They function as competent handlers, says Wamba-dia-Wamba, of

> dialectics; they are therefore dialecticians. . . . They are very able detectors of the divisive "bad word"—and stimulators of the palaver; they help assure that it does not degenerate into violent antagonism. They know how to make severe criticisms without offending or silencing the one criticized.[40]

Wamba-dia-Wamba goes on to note that a good *Nzonzi*

> must know how *to listen* attentively and tirelessly; *to pick up* the essence of each word spoken; *to observe* every look, every gesture, every silence; *to grasp* their respective significance . . . and to elaborate . . . arguments to counter . . . unjust positions and/or to re-affirm or reinforce correct positions.[41]

In a word, *Nzonzi* are like Socratic midwives, guiding the palaver to just and wise conclusions.[42] Furthermore, like the Ashanti consensual model of community governance, the village palaver in central Africa is an exceptionally democratic form of local governance.

A final example from our traditional African models that can inform our modern attempts to develop more deliberative democratic systems is provided by Mahmood Mamdani from yet another region of Africa, a Transkei-based community organization in South Africa. This example shows the difference between a "traditional chiefship in the preconquest period with the one under colonial rule." He writes:

> The traditional chief functioned in "an advisory and consultative context, unlike the bureaucratic model imposed under colonialism." The administrative power of such a chief consisted mainly in "the right to allocate land," but it was a right exercised through a double consultation: "with his (sometimes her) counselors, but primarily in consultation with the wider community," for the chief was "the custodian" of the land, not its proprietor. And custody "could only be exercised through a consensus of the community as a whole." The ultimate popular sanction against a despotic chief was desertion: "You tried to increase your following, rather than encouraging desertion to a neighboring chief, or to a rival relative." Colonial conquest built on the administrative powers of the chief, introducing "a highly bureaucratic command-and-control system." Under

apartheid, "the administrative powers of the chief were systematically strength-
ened" but were made accountable to "a new consensus" one that "emphasized
the state as the determiner of the consensus.⁴³

The point here, and in Botswana among Tswana and in the Kingdom of
Swaziland societies as well, is that through councils and a variety of peer
structures there were numerous checks and balances to a chief garnering too
much power and authority. Such public consensual forms of deliberation and
governance were systematically dismantled by colonial administrations.

I believe it is very clear that a modern democracy in Africa, in the sense of
rule of, by, and for the people requires that it be developed by the people and
engaged in through a highly deliberative process. To sustain a meaningful
modern democracy—even if "the majority decides," the "minority must be
respected." This requires three things: (1) appropriate, widespread participation or representation, (2) basic human rights be preserved for all, and (3) a
public political system of checks and balances that include an independent judiciary and freedom of the press to which those belonging to minorities have
no less access than those in power.⁴⁴ With all of this, we must see a modern
democracy in Africa as a process, growing from local roots and appropriating
deliberative forms appropriate to its civic development.

A central part of that process, especially that of respect for minorities, is
expressed very clearly by the American legal theorist Ronald Dworkin, in discussing the virtues of the highly regarded late American Justice, Learned
Hand, comments as follows. In order *to keep from suppressing minority expression,* "it is important that the public participate in the decisions [of the
community] not because the community should reach the decision *most people favor* [a majority decision], but for the very different reason that Hand
emphasized; that self-respect requires that people participate, as partners in a
joint venture, in the moral argument over the rules under which they live."⁴⁵
It is with this greater participatory sense that we can keep "our spirit of liberty alive" and develop "a national sense of justice." Such a democratic
process, says Dworkin, "engages us as moral deliberators and advocates
rather than just as numbers in a political count [or as a relatively insignificant
number in a majority vote]."⁴⁶

Dworkin puts forward his own version of deliberative democracy that
grows out of what he calls "a moral reading of the constitution." He argues
that implied in the American Constitution is the underlying assumption that
"government must treat all those subject to its dominion as having equal
moral and political status; it must attempt, in good faith, to treat them all with
equal concern; and it must respect whatever individual freedoms are indis-

pensable to those ends, including but not limited to the freedoms more specifically designated in the document, such as speech and religion."[47]

I believe there are similar underlying assumptions in the new South African Constitution that lend it to a "moral reading." Dworkin sees this assumption "of equal status for all" as posing an alternative to the majoritarian view of democracy. As a moral member of the community each citizen must have the opportunity to play a part in the community's life. Dworkin says: "Each person must have an opportunity to make a difference in the collective decisions" and that his or her role "must not be structurally fixed or limited in ways that reflect assumptions about his or her worth or talent or ability, or the soundness of his or her convictions or tastes."[48] Another important feature of moral membership, Dworkin says,

> involves reciprocity: a person is not a member unless he or she is treated as a member by others, which means that they treat the consequences of any collective decision for his or her life as equally significant a reason for or against that decision as are comparable consequences for the life of anyone else. So the communal conception of democracy explains an intuition many of us share: that a society in which the majority shows contempt for the needs and prospects of some minority is illegitimate as well as unjust.[49]

I believe there is a strong resemblance in this "moral reading" of Dworkin with the consensus/deliberative model of our African thinkers. In both, there must be *mutual* respect (reciprocity) and any minority community must equally benefit from collective decisions of the government. This is a central moral and political feature of any democratic community that wants to lay claim to being a just community.

We must finally distinguish the virtues of a "deliberative democracy" from the contemporary versions of what is called "liberal democracy." There is a litany of voices that cry out against "liberal democracy"—many in favor of some form or another of communitarian thinking and traditionalism.[50] These critics argue that liberal democracy has erred in the direction of a fragmented individualism and a legal overemphasis on "rights." Deliberative democracy, contrary to the perceived notion of liberal democracy, is understood to depend upon particular communities and their traditional values where each person becomes who he or she can be through the reciprocal valuing and criticizing of others in their community. This is precisely what is meant by Stanley Cavell's idea of the "virtue of responsiveness" that opened this book. Such responsiveness provides a foundation for understanding justice. On a broader scale this responsive deliberative process can also take place between communities or cultures, where reasons are given and listened to in support of one's values. Deliberative democracy both within a community or tradition and between them presupposes a process of reciprocity in its struggles toward a just civic order for all of its members. Within a number of traditional African societies, as we have seen, there are certain fundamental moral concepts like *"ubuntu"* that may underlie the way communities shape their democratic processes and their very conception of justice.

Generally, the moral end of justice in any democratic society is for its people to treat one another decently and to insure its social order and peaceful survival. This may appear to be a modest claim, but not an easy one to realize, especially when a robust—or thick—ideal of justice is at the center of its virtues for a democratic society. When such a view of justice is at the center, the expectations of the peoples' practices are raised. "Decent" treatment of others means that one is obliged to treat them with dignity and respect. This expectation may often be where "others" include a diversity of cultures and religious beliefs. Here, of course, trust is an essential component in people's day-to-day practices, and cultivating a capacity for sympathetic understanding of others contributes to civic harmony. It also means that the foundations for the law to maintain civic order must be such as to preserve the dignity *for all* regardless of differences in culture and religious beliefs. It is in this second aspect of a democratic society, its legal systems, that a just system may best be served with "restorative" means and ends in mind for sustaining its civic order. Thus virtues of mercy, compassion, and reconciliation should follow from the mutual trust and understanding of its citizens.

The very idea of "justice," therefore, should embrace those virtues or moral practices of trust, mutual understanding, mercy, compassion, and reconciliation. None of these practices, in themselves, rules out the need for various forms of criminal and civil punishment for crimes that will be committed. These practices, however, do entail the development and nurturing of *a greater deliberative public culture* to sustain a peaceful order, especially in societies with a large diversity of cultures and beliefs. It is, of course, for just such pluralistic societies, that deliberative democracies are best suited. To paraphrase John Dunn: It might simply be true that human beings now cannot learn to live together in a more deliberative manner, and even with such counter evidence as is provided by the South African experience and elsewhere, human beings may believe that forgiveness and reconciliation go against our instinctive grain. But that does not mean that if we really tried to engage in more deliberative practices, to promote a justice that aims at moral outcomes, to be more responsive to other human beings, and to seek greater reconciliation among our selves, that we could not achieve greater peace and justice in our human communities around the world.

A deliberative democracy requires first lifting a community from poverty and oppressive governance and restoring the people's dignity. A deliberative democracy anchors each citizen in everyday life, and gives each person a voice in, and some responsibility for, their own well-being and the flourishing of their community. It requires the development of the proper "habits of mind" as Wiredu said. A deliberative democracy also requires a *cooperative democratic partnership* between local communities, connecting NGOs with both their service toward the communities and their lobbying skills with governments and global institutions like World Bank, micro-lending agencies, human rights organizations, and agricultural, business, and environmental development agencies.

These examples from several continents, regarding deliberative democracy should all be part of the process of promoting justice—a justice that encourages greater human reflections and participation in civic life and also a justice that promotes greater moral outcomes such as respect for human rights and human reconciliation. In this framework I would define justice as follows: *Justice is the principle moral virtue for organizing human communities that enables the maximum of human freedom and dignity and that recognizes when harm arises or inequities endure, deliberative measures must be taken to restore a peaceful and equitable balance.* Furthermore, as part of a just human community we are, in the words of Simone Weil, "obliged to safeguard the autonomy of others." A justice that embraces both these "restorative" and "deliberative" virtues protects not only human rights, but obliges individuals and communities to take responsibility for the well being of all of its members.

NOTES

1. Jonathan Sacks, *The Dignity of Difference*, 178f.
2. As found in Sacks, *The Dignity of Difference*, 187.
3. Sacks, *The Dignity of Difference*, 186f.
4. For a wider discussion of this point see Martha Minow, *Between Vengeance and Forgiveness,* and Priscilla B. Hayner, *Unspeakable Truths: Confronting State Terror and Atrocity.*
5. John Braithwaite, *Restorative Justice and Responsive Regulation* (Oxford: Oxford University Press, 2002), 5.
6. Wilhelm Verwoerd, "Individual and/or Social Justice after Apartheid?" *The European Journal of Development Research* 11, no. 2 (December 1999): 124.
7. Verwoerd, "Individual and/or Social Justice after Apartheid?" 124.
8. John Braithwaite, *Restorative Justice and Responsive Regulation*, 134.

9. John Braithwaite, *Restorative Justice and Responsive Regulation*. Braithwaite has also edited two volumes with Heather Strang that collect a dozen or more essays from around the globe on various aspects of "restorative justice." See their *Restorative Justice and Civil Society* (Cambridge: Cambridge University Press, 2001) and *Restorative Justice: Philosophy to Practice* (London and Burlington, VT: Ashgate Publishing Co., 2000).

10. Braithwaite, *Restorative Justice and Responsive Regulation*, viii.

11. Braithwaite, *Restorative Justice and Responsive Regulation*, x.

12. Braithwaite and Strang (eds.) in *Restorative Justice and Civil Society*, call attention to the social science classic *Making Democracy Work: Civic Traditions in Modern Italy* (1993) by Robert Putnam. "Putnam has been able to show that the direction of historical causality operating here is not that economic success generates a trust-based culture but that a strong fabric of trust, woven in institutions of civil society, has economic benefits," 5. Braithwaite and Strang also call attention to how emotion links to restorative values: "A thread running through our chapters is that the power of restorative justice may be connected to the fact that it does not subordinate emotion to dispassionate justice. . . . Space is created in civil society for the free expression of emotions, however irrational they may seem . . . of course, civil society will not produce a civil society unless there is civility—mutual respect and non-violence—in how emotions are conveyed," 10.

13. For details of these reparations and others see Priscilla Hayner, *Unspeakable Truths*, 170–182. Hayner characterizes reparations as follows: "*Reparations* is a general term that encompasses a variety of types of redress, including *restitution, compensation, rehabilitation, satisfaction, and guarantees of nonrepetition*," 171.

14. Braithwaite, *Restorative Justice and Responsive Regulation*, 69.

15. Braithwaite, *Restorative Justice and Responsive Regulation,* 129. My emphasis.

16. Braithwaite, *Restorative Justice and Responsive Regulation*, 126.

17. A phrase used by David Burrell in a lecture, "Faith, Culture, and Reason" at the College of Wooster, November 10, 2003.

18. Braithwaite, *Restorative Justice and Responsive Regulation,* 127.

19. However quickly the conflict may come to some stability, there is no doubt that it exacerbated retributive violence to the extent of greater suffering to Iraqi citizens and greater than expected death and casualties to American soldiers and allied personnel.

20. As found in Braithwaite, *Restorative Justice and Responsive Regulation,* 126. My emphasis.

21. Braithwaite and Strang, *Restorative Justice and Civil Society,* 1.

22. Braithwaite and Strang, *Restorative Justice and Civil Society*, 37.

23. From research essay "Restorative Justice, Amnesty, and the Creation of the New South Africa," by Debra Dalton for my graduate seminar in "African Philosophy" at Rhodes University, Grahamstown, South Africa, October 2004, 8.

24. Braithwaite, *Restorative Justice and Responsive Regulation,* 129. My emphasis.

25. Wilhelm Verwoerd walks us through that case in his unpublished essay "Amnesty and Mercy" (2002). This is also evident in the scenes from and testimony

of the Biehls and the perpetrators documented in the film "Long Night's Journey into Day."

26. Wilhelm Verwoerd, "Amnesty and Mercy" unpublished manuscript text, 50.

27. This account is in an unpublished meditation written by Wilhelm Verwoerd "A Face of Forgiveness" (2003).

Several acts of forgiveness have surrounded the imprisoned Eugene de Kock and families of persons he had killed or injured. See Pumla Gobodo-Mandikizela, *A Human Being Died That Night: A South African Story of Forgiveness*, see chapters 4 through 7.

28. Jonathan Sacks, *The Dignity of Difference*, 179.

29. A remark of K. Pranis, "A State Initiative toward Restorative Justice: The Minnesota Experience," as found in Braithwaite, *Restorative Justice and Responsive Regulation*, 133.

30. Braithwaite, *Restorative Justice and Responsive Regulation*, 131.

31. Kwasi Wiredu, "Democracy by Consensus: Some Conceptual Considerations" in a special issue of *Philosophical Papers,* 30, no. 3, (November 2001), edited by Richard H. Bell.

32. Wiredu, "Democracy by Consensus," 244. My emphasis.

33. See several essays of Wiredu, e.g., "Democracy and Consensus" in *Cultural Universals and Particulars: An African Perspective* (Bloomington: Indiana University Press, 1996), 186ff, and "Democracy by Consensus: Some Conceptual Considerations," in a special issue of *Philosophical Papers,* 227–44.

34. Kwasi Wiredu, "The State, Civil Society and Democracy in Africa," *Quest* 12, no. 1 (1998): 250. We only have to think of Zimbabwe during the past decade.

Such "instability" and "failures" in African transitions from colonial rule to some "near" democratic status is clearly set forward in the recent study of transitions made in French West Africa since the 1960s. See *Not Yet Democracy: West Africa's Slow Farewell to Authoritarianism,* by Boubacar N'Daye, Abdoulaye Saine, and Mathurin Hounjgnikpo (Durham, NC: Carolina Academic Press, 2005).

See also Elias K. Bongmba, *The Dialectics of Transformation in Africa* (New York: Palgrave Macmillan, 2006). See especially his Chapter 2, "The Genesis of the African Crisis: The Manifestation of a Political Will," 39–62.

35. Mahmood Mamdani, *Citizen and Subject: Contemporary Africa and the Legacy of Late Colonialism* (Princeton: Princeton University Press, 1996), 45ff.

36. Wiredu, *Cultural Universals,* 187. There are many good examples of this democratic model by consensus. I have discussed other variations dealing with African democracy in village life in my book *Understanding African Philosophy: A Cross-Cultural Approach to Classical and Contemporary Issues* (New York: Routledge, 2002), especially chapters 4 and 6. Examples are the consensus democratic model of village palavers in Central Africa provided by Ernest Wamba-dia-Wamba, and local governance structures in West Africa discussed by Kwame Gyekye leading to a moderate communitarian view of civic order.

37. Gyekye, *Tradition and Modernity,* 116ff.

38. E. Wamba-dia-Wamba, "Experience of Democracy in Africa: Reflections on Practices of Communalistic Palaver as a Social Method of Resolving Contradictions

among the People." A paper discussed in a Seminar in the Department of Theory and History of State Law, Faculty of Law, University of Dar es Salaam, May 17, 1985, 5. Unpublished. Wamba-dia-Wamba is a Congolese historian and philosopher who has taught at the University of Dar es Salaam for the past decade or so. In 1999 he returned to the Congo to head up a faction of "rebels" against the Laurent Kabila government.

39. Wamba-dia-Wamba, "Experience of Democracy," 24f.
40. Wamba-dia-Wamba, "Experience of Democracy," 30.
41. Wamba-dia-Wamba, "Experience of Democracy," 31. My emphasis.
42. Wamba-dia-Wamba, "Experience of Democracy," 32f.
43. Mahmood Mamdani, *Citizen and Subject*, 45. Further examples of what Benjamin R. Barber calls "strong democracy" can be found in his *Strong Democracy: Participatory Politics for a New Age* (Berkeley: University of California Press, 1984). See especially 150–155.
44. A similar point has been made by Bas de Gaay Forman in his essay "Conceptualizing Democracy in an African Context," *Quest* 8, no. 1 (June 1994): 68–69.
45. Dworkin, *Freedom's Law*, 344. My emphasis and bracketed inserts.
46. Dworkin, *Freedom's Law*, 346f.
47. Dworkin, *Freedom's Law*, 8.
48. Dworkin, *Freedom's Law*, 24.
49. Dworkin, *Freedom's Law*, 25.
50. See works by Alasdair MacIntyre and Stanley Hauerwas among others. Their views and others in this discussion are also reviewed and criticized by Jeffrey Stout in his *Democracy and Tradition* (2004).

Chapter Seven

Justice and Spirituality:
A Testament to Our Humanity

True goodness, true responsibility, true justice, a true sense of things—all these grow from roots that go much deeper than the world of our transitory earthly schemes. This is a message that speaks to us from the very heart of human [spirituality].

[Vaclav Havel, Hiroshima, Japan, August 1995]

SPIRITUALITY'S LINK WITH JUSTICE

How does the notion of the "spiritual" or "spirituality" inform our discussion of justice? Why should we link justice with the concept of spirituality? The concept of spirituality was naturally placed—in a rather unannounced manner—into our discussion in the introduction with John Dunn's lament about "modern philosophical theories of justice [being] simply idle: practically inert." He decried the inattention to the "moral, spiritual or aesthetic aspirations" of human beings in our thinking about justice. In fact, in evoking the trilogy of concepts—moral, spiritual, or aesthetic—each of which are supposed to lay on the "other side" of our intellectual, objective pursuits of scientific knowledge, Dunn highlights our need to return them to the fray; to the ground of our human condition. We must not turn our eyes from the *injustices* we find in this world.

Justice, as Vaclav Havel notes above, "grow[s] from roots that go much deeper than the world of our transitory earthly schemes. . . . [it] speaks to us from the very heart of human spirituality." Justice begins the moment we "face" our neighbor and accept responsibility for his or her humanity. We should, as Thoreau advised, approach justice with a certain stillness or presence to our human political condition and recall ourselves to ourselves in a kind of truthfulness that can awaken us from vengeful and self-serving patterns of living.

Because of the difficulty of being just we often look beyond ourselves for help. It is here that the notion of the spiritual surfaces and that spirituality interfaces with justice. There are, however, numerous pitfalls in the contemporary uses of the word "spirituality." Lawyer-theologian William Stringfellow was skeptical regarding the term spirituality and cautioned us about its use. He insisted that the word "spirituality" be understood "free of the voguish, supercilious, commercialized, or religiose contexts"[1] in which it is too often invoked—or what he called the "clutter" associated with the term "spirituality."[2] In contrast to these modalities, Stringfellow saw the concept of spirituality linked to the notion of "holiness," and said being holy is

> being whole . . . it means being liberated from religiosity and religious piety of any sort; it does not mean being morally better, it means being exemplary; it does not mean being godly, but rather being truly human; it does not mean being other worldly, but it means being deeply implicated in the practical existence of this world without succumbing to this world.[3]

Stringfellow also wanted us to see the concept of spirituality as meaningful only "in the midst of the Fall," that is, as a means of directly and humanly confronting the harm, oppressive acts and injustices that humans inflict upon one another, and in transforming one's relationships with other human beings into concrete acts of reconciliation. This sense of spirituality he said "is thus *the most profoundly political reality available to human experience.*"[4] What he then called "the politics of spirituality" is the engagement with the world that involves the whole person in a manner that transforms the world through a kind of justice as compassion and reconciliation—a kind of struggle for justice that Simone Weil called an incarnate love of the world, a "mad love." *Such a politics Stringfellow called "a spiritual disposition" or "practice," and he considered this "the most radical politics of all."*[5]

A central feature of Stringfellow's link between spirituality and justice is how "a person enters a sense of moral worthiness."[6] Such worthiness is a release from power and self-indulgence to a form of life shaped by humility and kindness. This moral worthiness or "ethics" as Levinas noted, is "probably the very spirituality of the soul." Justice, understood "spiritually," is a gift of the practice of love and reconciliation with your neighbors and distant strangers, it is "being holy" in a "fallen" world. Insofar as such a witness is absent, Stringfellow believed, *injustice* will prevail.

Justice requires that we reestablish certain moral qualities that have given it its primacy among the virtues. These qualities include trust, obligation, equality and mutual respect, mercy and forgiveness, compassion, and reconciliation. These are qualities fundamentally intrinsic to our humanity, even as they have been challenged and suppressed by fear, injustice, and vengeance in the tyrannies and terrible acts of human beings and by the powers and principalities of this world. We have seen these qualities of the virtue of justice present in the heart of the *Iliad*, in Socrates and Seneca, in Levinas and Simone Weil, in Nussbaum and Sen, as well as in the myriad acts of kindness and care visible in the lives of ordinary human beings struggling to live with dignity and decency toward their fellow human beings.

The idea of "our humanity" does not, however, lead us directly to a particular view of a God, nor is there a sudden awareness of some anonymous secular idea of what it is to be a human being. We learn our sectarian/religious views or our secular views of what living as a human being means from our cultures (small and large), our religious or non-religious training, and our daily moral and social practices. It is not as if humanity—that is, our awareness of being human—emerged into its present self-consciousness *as* a Jew, a pagan, a Christian, a Taoist, a Muslim, a Hindu, a Buddhist, or as a "modern" secular rationalist or skeptic. The process of coming to awareness of our humanity—of coming to a particular self-consciousness with others—is first a gradual recognition of our being present *with* others.

We do not just happen upon the idea of justice either. But something like the idea of justice either precedes or is conjoined with a growing consciousness of why and what it means to be who we are *with others*; of how we are to manage our lives in the presence of—or face to face—with others. Our very survival becomes an exercise in trust, in social balance, in reciprocity and responsiveness, and finally in the recognition of responsibility *for* others. In fact, the very notion of being *obligated* to someone else arises before we can make any claims for ourselves. Self-concern is moderated by those who have nurtured us and also by those with whom we have to live.

The evocation of some spiritual aspiration, some concept of God, of "Fall" and "Grace," some sense of transcendence, some sense of presence in a vast universe, arises *after* we are aware of our humanity. We can only put the idea of our humanity together with our primitive patterns of behavior if we have some point of reference outside ourselves. This is where the notion of a spiritual aspiration arises—at the point where we reflect upon ourselves in the act of being human *with others*. Or, as Anthony Bloom said, my acting moral or just toward others "begins at the moment when I see my neighbor (individual or collective) as different from me, at times irreducibly different, and recognizing his total right to be so, accept the fact that he is himself and has no reason to be merely a replica of myself."[7]

There is "a true sense of things," Havel said, "that speaks to us from the very heart of human spirituality." This is what I would call a kind of "natural spirituality"[8]—a spirituality that arises from the human heart and that need not be linked with a particular kind of theism or even a notion of "God." Generally, the idea of spirituality evokes how a sense of the sacred either breaks out from within the human heart (natural spirituality), or how the sacred breaks into the ordinary of human life (a kind of incarnational spirituality). Both kinds of spirituality have links with justice, with how we develop a sense of moral worthiness in community, with how each person lives toward another person in this world.

This point is precisely stated in Simone Weil's remark cited in Chapter 5, above. She wrote: "What we need is a spirit of justice to dwell within us. The spirit of justice is nothing other than the supreme and perfect flower of the madness of love." Such "madness" underscores a natural passion to identify our humanity within each human being—whether that humanity is understood to be divinely or otherwise created. To exemplify these two kinds of spirituality linked with justice we will briefly look at ideas found in Vaclav Havel and Simone Weil.

JUSTICE AND "THE ABSOLUTE HORIZON OF BEING"

Vaclav Havel has an unusual clarity in writing about his particular human condition and how he came to his own awareness of his humanity. He understands intuitively what having his freedom denied means for his very being, and how the human condition of his fellow Czech citizens, denied their dignity, destroys their humanity. He zeroes in, on the one hand, on what undermines the most important of human virtues: justice and compassion. On the other hand, he emphasizes what constitutes his very humanity within an "horizon of Being."

Embodied in the story of the people's long struggle toward a just society in Czechoslovakia during the last half of the twentieth century is a sense of justice bounded by an expanding horizon of humanity; a sense of justice that embraces truth-telling, a deliberative process that is symbolized by silent dissent, a public refusal to lie, and a belief in friendship and compassion. It is a struggle that requires a certain "spiritual and moral condition" that puts humanity in touch with what Havel calls "the miracle of Being." Let us look briefly at how he came to embrace this miracle.

In an open letter to his country's president, Dr. Gustav Husak, in 1975, Havel speaks of the utter "humiliation" suffered every day by the Czech and Slovak people by virtue of their being forced "to live a lie." He says, "People have a very acute appreciation of the price they have paid for outward peace and quiet: the permanent *humiliation of their human dignity*."[9] He describes this humiliation of human dignity in great detail with concrete examples in this letter and in his better-known essay "The Power of the Powerless" (1978).[10] What prevails, he says, is "*order without life*": "Order has been established at the price of a paralysis of the spirit, a deadening of the heart, and devastation of life. Surface 'consolidation' has been achieved at the price of a *spiritual and moral crisis in society*."[11] What does a human being need to overcome such a crisis? Clearly finding a way of life that *is* spiritual, that expresses one's moral worthiness, and that restores a meaningful sense of life!

It is important to detail Havel's view to show that his "spiritual reading" of morality and politics is not an anomaly even at the beginning of the twenty-first century; it is an illustration that Enlightenment morality and politics can be effectively challenged by rebellious, yet practical, civic leaders at the present hour. Havel had reflectively developed this vision of a spiritual and a just moral life through his long and active struggle against his government. During one of his stays in prison, between June 1979 and September 1982, he articulated his maturing moral and political views in letters to his wife, Olga. In these letters he is in search of what he calls "the absolute horizon of all life's relativities"—of which, he says, "many experience as God" (November 1980).[12] This idea of an "absolute horizon" is rather imprecise in his early letters but becomes increasingly clear as he tries to relate it to human action, to moral responsibility, and to politics. Although not experienced "as God" by Havel, he discovers this horizon to be "that before which we should bow down humbly because of the mystery about it"—the horizon in which "justice, honor, treason, friendship, infidelity, courage or empathy have a wholly tangible content." This horizon "grounds, delimits, animates and directs" our natural world. To Olga he says, "there can be no transitory human existence without the horizon of permanence against which it develops and to which . . . it constantly relates" (January 1981).[13] This provides a normative framework that gives meaning to why human beings feel "obliged" to act on others' behalf, why we take responsibility for our neighbor or assist a stranger in need.

Within the next year he would write to Olga that this "absolute horizon" is "the only source of our hope, the only 'reason' for faith as a (consciously reflected) state of mind . . .; that it "evokes the hope that [life] actually does have meaning, encourages one to live, helps one resist the feeling that all is vanity and futility, the pressure of nothingness."[14] The search for the meaning of life is a constant "striving for something beyond us and above us," something to hold on to, but in the striving we discover that it is also "holding on to us."[15]

By spring of 1982, a friend had hand-copied in a letter several essays of Emmanuel Levinas and smuggled them into prison. Havel's letters from that point reflect a focused concern with a sense of obligation, a moral responsibility, and an ethic of love of neighbor (ideas central to Levinas' thought) as this links to the notion of an "absolute horizon." He learns from Levinas that we establish our identity when we "face" another and become responsible; thus our human social and political lives are constituted in our moral practices. He asks himself the question: "What does 'responsibility' mean . . . responsibility not only to the world, but also 'for the world,' . . . Whence comes this strange and clearly impractical . . . essence of the moral law, that which is called 'good'?" He thinks the answer is clear:

> That curious feeling of "responsibility for the world" can probably only be felt by someone who is really (consciously or unconsciously) in touch, within himself, with "the absolute horizon of Being," who communicates or struggles with it in some way, who draws from it meaning, hope and faith, who has genuinely (through inner experience) grasped it. . . . In other words: by perceiving ourselves as part of the river, we accept our responsibility for the river as a whole. . . . (March 1982)[16]

Havel's last reflections move closer to how a person is to act in the concrete world—in accepting "responsibility for the river as a whole." Here he moves closer to Levinas and Levinas' mentor Martin Buber. Havel writes:

> In the nearness of love of another [the I] comes to know its home; . . . In short, in the experience of the other it experiences everything that it means to be human: . . . *Face-to-face with the existence of his neighbor, he first experiences the primordial "responsibility for everything" and thus becomes a special creature capable of fellow feeling with a complete stranger,* of loving even that which he does not erotically desire or on whom he is not dependent for his existence-in-the-world.

He concludes that "a better outlook for human communality" lies in "love, charity, sympathy, tolerance, understanding, self-control, solidarity, friendship, feelings of belonging, the acceptance of concrete responsibility for those close to one" (August 28, 1982).[17] These remarks embrace a "complete" concept of justice; they reflect our "moral worthiness" and our responsibility to humanity.

Havel affirms that whatever practices one chooses they must be understood within some spiritual frame, "placed against the background of an horizon," which give them their meaning and authority and keep them from becoming, in the words of Jean Bethke Elshtain, "latter-day Protagorean efforts to make man the measure of all things."[18]

Finally, Havel says the task for a meaningful moral and political life, both East and West, should be

> one of resisting vigilantly, thoughtfully and attentively, but at the same time with total dedication, at every step and everywhere, the irrational momentum of anonymous, impersonal and inhuman power. . . . We must resist their complex and wholly alienating pressure, . . . [and] honor with the humility of the wise the bounds of that natural world and the mystery which lies beyond them.[19]

Havel's words and deeds are a testament to our humanity in a clear, unequivocal way. Human decency and communality, civic order and responsibility, humility, hope, and human compassion are all understood by Havel in a framework or horizon of the spirit. As recently at 1994, in a speech in Philadelphia, Havel reaffirmed his spiritual vision of justice. He said:

> The only real hope of people today is probably a renewal of our certainty that we are rooted in the Earth and at the same time, the cosmos. This awareness endows us with the capacity for self-transcendence.
>
> Politicians at international forums may reiterate a thousand times that the basis of the new world order must be universal respect for human rights, but it will mean nothing as long as this imperative does not derive from the respect of the miracle of Being, the miracle of the universe, the miracle of nature, the miracle of our own existence. Only someone who submits to the authority of the universal order and of creation, who values the right to be a part of it and a participant in it, can genuinely value himself and his neighbors and thus honor their rights as well.[20]

Havel understood that these features of a civil society required a concept of justice and a legal system that was ennobled by the absolute horizon of Being and a justice that would ennoble the human spirit.

Havel did not need a formal traditional religious faith to understand the meaning of justice. Rather, he found a way to articulate a belief in his own humanity and a kind of justice that would surface with the recognition that he was not alone in this belief. Havel's life and liberating words; his humanizing conception of justice embodies the best of what political theorist John Dunn called the moral, aesthetic, and spiritual aspirations of humanity. Havel could not have succeeded had he sought to fight for a retributive kind of justice; it was not a simple matter of rebalancing the scales and articulating what was his "due" or the "just deserts" of his offended fellow citizens. He had to cultivate and count on a new or renewed virtue of justice *as* compassion; he had to "re-call" a spirit of forgiveness and reconciliation to avoid sustaining cycles of revenge. In his testament to our humanity, Havel provides us with what I would call a disciplined, democratic and compassionate "spirit" turned into *a new kind of human spirituality and justice.*[21]

SPIRITUALITY AND JUSTICE IN SIMONE WEIL

Simone Weil's view of spirituality's link with justice is different in important ways from Havel's. On the one hand there is a more explicit "religious" aspect to her account, while on the other hand, her view is not tied to a single specific religious faith. One could call her "explicit religious" idea of justice "incarnational" and thereby distinguishing it from Havel's natural spirituality. Weil understood the idea of God found in all religions as well as in classical Greek thought as "incarnational"—a way in which God insinuates God's self into this world. She draws from many spiritual sources, Christianity, Old Testament prophetic literature, pre-Socratic Greek literature, and what she calls "Oriental thought" including *The Egyptian Book of the Dead*, The *Bhagavad-Gita*, and Taoism. There is also a strong "rational" strain in her thinking about justice that enables her to challenge other modern post-Enlightenment views and then go beyond them.

In Simone Weil we find a concept of justice that she called a new virtue—a "supernatural" or spiritual virtue—that challenges the political philosophies of our time. Without denying the importance in our thinking and our moral practice of "human rational agency" she is clear in arguing that justice cannot rest on such human rational agency alone. Justice, she says, is a "beautiful" word with "a power infinitely greater than any human conception."[22] This moves her beyond the modern liberal and secular views and forces new angles of vision on our rethinking of justice. Briefly, this new concept of justice is based on the awareness of a *disequilibrium* of power in the world and not on assuming a balance of power.

Justice for Simone Weil requires that we think in a new way; that we adopt a perspective that can counterbalance the *realpolitik*. This requires a "supernatural" or spiritual way of thinking about justice. Ultimately, she argues, justice is beyond human control to "balance the scales" in our human world. Justice requires some quality of supernatural intervention. For her, then, we must think about justice from a perspective that is outside the world but that finds its operational axis within the world.[23]

This *new* virtue of justice, embraces (a) a human capacity for attention to injustice (as discussed earlier), (b) that we harm no one (as in Socrates), (c) nor return evil for evil (as Jesus commands), and (d) that we act without arrogance or expectation of favor (against egoism). "Humanism," she remarked, "was not wrong in thinking that [truth, beauty and love] are of infinite value, but in thinking that man can get them for himself without grace."[24] To think we can get justice without grace is to remove the term from its spiritual order; it is to renounce its "beauty."

This is clearly *a very radical formulation of what justice is* considering the nearly 300 years that have been spent on the "modern," secular formulations within which we operate in Western democracies. If, however, we go back to Socrates, Lao-tzu, and Confucius, and even earlier to the *Iliad* and Egyptian concerns with harm and hunger, their desire for homecomings and hot baths, where balance, harmony, and peaceableness (*ataraxia*) are our chief aim both personally and publicly, then Simone Weil's struggle to give us a *spiritual* reading of justice does not appear quite so radical or novel an idea. Add to this the Incarnation where God descends to suffer humiliation and affliction, and the Gospel obligation—the message of unconditional love of neighbor—Simone Weil brings forward a radical spiritual vision of justice.[25]

In her later reflections, Simone Weil goes so far as to say that there is "no distinction between love of our neighbor and justice."[26] In fact she says: "Only the absolute identification of justice and love makes the coexistence possible of compassion and gratitude on the one hand, and on the other, of respect for the dignity of affliction in the afflicted—a respect felt by the sufferer himself and the others."[27] The important feature in what is an asymmetrical aspect of justice is that "the supernatural virtue of justice consists of *behaving exactly as though there were equality* when one is the stronger in an unequal relationship."[28] Thus, if you are in a position of power or control or wealth relative to another human being, there must be mutual consent between the parties, and the weaker party should in no way feel humiliated, or the stronger superior. The fact will remain, however, that the condition of inequality will persist by necessity. That is why a "supernatural" virtue is required to bring about justice.

This asymmetrical view is summed up in a passage that predates Levinas' view of ethics by several decades—the view that ethics has its foundation in "the face" of the other—Simone Weil wrote:

> In true love it is not we who love the afflicted in God; it is God in us who loves them. When we are in affliction, it is God in us who loves those who wish us well. *Compassion and gratitude come down from God, and when they are exchanged in a glance, God is present at the point where the eyes of those who give and those who receive meet.* The sufferer and the other love each other, starting from God through God, but not for the love of God; they love each other for the love of the one for the other. This is an impossibility. That is why it comes about only through the agency of God.[29]

To understand this remark with all its radical spiritual implications is a key to understanding Simone Weil's new virtue of justice.

The whole notion of justice is transformed into a new spiritual virtue when viewed on this cosmic, supernatural scale. We will not, according to Simone Weil, "naturally" move in a benevolent or sacrificial manner to preserve the good against what she calls "necessity" or "gravity." The sooner we recognize our human limitations, the greater becomes the prospect of being open to grace or "the agency of God" in every act of justice toward those whose eyes we meet.

She sees this factor as implicit in every culture around the globe—historically and contemporaneously. "Grace," she says, "is the law of descending movement. An ascending movement is natural, a descending one supernatural."[30] This formulation of justice in terms of grace is hardly bizarre. It appears so only against the Enlightenment background of modern political thought where all is conceived solely in terms of "human rational agency"—an "ascending order" with progress in mind.

One of the strongest statements in Simone Weil's writings that resolves this asymmetry between God and grace, on the one hand, and our human world of necessity on the other hand, is her belief in justice as an act of *compassion shown in the human world*. She writes:

> God is absent from this world, except in the existence in this world of those in whom His love is alive. Therefore they [we human beings] ought to be present in the world through compassion. Their compassion is the visible presence of God here below.
>
> When we are lacking in compassion we make a violent separation between a creature and God.
>
> Through compassion we can put the created, temporal part of a creature in communication with God. . . .
>
> Compassion is what spans this abyss which creation has opened between God and the creature.
>
> Compassion is the rainbow.[31]

Justice as compassion is what spans the abyss that creation opened between God and humanity. It is in, and only in, our acts of love and justice toward the other, that God's love is shown to be alive.

We have in Vaclav Havel and in Simone Weil, two ways of talking about spirituality and justice in contemporary society. The first is, as Havel says, to speak from the very heart of the human spirit or from "human spirituality." Here the understanding of our human nature, as Havel said, is that our humanity goes beyond "our transitory earthly schemes"; that the human spirit cannot be bound by our common earthly concerns, but has a capacity to transcend its own ordinary limits and see itself as part of one's neighbor as well as having meaning with the larger global scheme of things. The human spirit has a capacity to effect change within larger human contexts and to allow human beings in any and every context in which they find themselves, for better or worse, to transcend, to go deeper into themselves, and to reflect the humanity that is every woman's and man's to express. Without linking this spirit to a particular sectarian God, Havel evokes the idea that "the meaning of any phenomenon lies in its being achieved in something outside itself" or in "the absolute horizon of our Being."

The second way of conceiving spirituality and justice assumes the first sense of some grounded or framed human spirit and then builds upon it. It offers a different explanation for the horizon of our Being. Anthony Bloom said that justice goes further and claims more from us. Justice begins, he says, "at the moment when I see my neighbor" and furthermore recognizes my neighbor "as different from me"—that my neighbor is not a mere "replica of myself." Beyond this recognition or our mutual, though different, humanity is the recognition that each of us is a creation of a higher being; that the other, my neighbor, is "not made in my image but in God's." This recognition adds a dimension of awe for humanity itself; it calls forth stillness, a silence, a respect that demands our being present to all that is created by God. Here we have a more theological configuration of spirituality and an expectation that justice itself is derived from a spiritual source outside ourselves though given expression through our acts of compassion toward other human beings. We have seen how Simone Weil accounts for this stillness and how it is linked to her "new virtue of justice"—a virtue that would be empty without Grace, without the notion of *God in us* and through whom we see our neighbor as the human being he or she is.

Finally, we could think of *justice spiritually* as a Carthusian monk recently did. He remarked: "The spiritual life is like a dance with a partner who has a fertile imagination and who leads. We must be alert, responsive to the slightest indication of his intention, supple, ready to adapt to the movements with which he woos us."[32] The partners in the dance of justice and spirituality are your fellows in humanity that you "go up to" or "face"—they are your neighbors in humanity, a friend or a distant stranger that you engage within some "horizon of Being" or in the presence of God. In this dance, justice demands we engage a partner with a certain kind of responsiveness; a responsiveness that is supple and sensitive; that treats the other with respect—as a brother or sister in humanity. In this partnership are all the themes we have set out in earlier chapters: responsiveness (Cavell and Levinas), attention and compassion (Simone Weil), responsibility and obligation (O'Neill and Havel), and mercy and forgiveness (Seneca, Nussbaum, Sacks, and numerous victims of apartheid's evils). All these play an important role in the spiritual partnership that is justice.

We come back now to where we began our conversation, to Thoreau's remark that we "only need sit still" and all in our present surrounding will "exhibit itself to us by turns." We have throughout this book been present to and responsive to varied "turns" or aspects of the concept of justice. We have been trying to discern all that is found in the concept of justice that pertains to individual and communal expectations within a civil society: mutual respect, compassion, and a concern for reconciliation. Such a presence to justice also requires a deliberate and deliberative attitude toward causes of injustice among human beings in order to restore a sense of civic order and responsibility. Such a presence in civic life is best found in a form of a deliberative democratic society.

It should be clear from the beginning of our journey—from Homer and Aeschylus, Socrates, and Seneca to more recent conversations on rights and obligations, on retributive and restorative justice—that justice is neither simply a political concept nor only a modern secular idea. It is a deeply human concept. Justice is a testament to our humanity, not an individual demand for compensation or "getting one's due." As a human concept, justice reminds us of our presence in the world with others, of "the face of the other" and of some greater "horizon of Being" or of the very being of a God. Justice reminds us of the concerns we share with all human beings. Furthermore, *justice reminds us that we have an obligation—a responsibility—to foster peace, to be merciful, and to promote reconciliation with our brothers and sisters in humanity. These are all essential to rethinking justice and to restoring our humanity.* Justice moves us beyond the secular—the "idle," "inert," and destructive spaces of a retributive attitude—and embraces the "spiritual aspirations" of humanity for greater hope, compassion, and cooperation across boundaries.

NOTES

1. William Stringfellow, *The Politics of Spirituality* (Philadelphia: The Westminster Press, 1984), 15.

2. Stringfellow itemizes "the clutter" as follows: "Spirituality may indicate stoic attitudes, occult phenomena, the practice of so-called mind control, yoga discipline, escapist fantasies, interior journeys, an appreciation of Eastern religions, multifarious pietistic exercises, superstitious imaginations, intensive journals, dynamic muscle tension, assorted dietary regimens, meditation, jogging cults, monastic rigors, mortification of the flesh, wilderness sojourns, political resistance, contemplation, abstinence, hospitality, a vocation of poverty, nonviolence, silence, the efforts of prayer, obedience, generosity, exhibiting stigmata, entering solitude, or, I suppose, among these and many other things, squatting on top of a pillar." *The Politics of Spirituality*, 19f.

3. Stringfellow, *The Politics of Spirituality,* 32.

4. Stringfellow, *The Politics of Spirituality*, 21. My emphasis.

5. Stringfellow, *The Politics of Spirituality*, 45.

6. Stringfellow, *The Politics of Spirituality*, 47.

7. Richard H. Bell and Barbara L. Battin, *Seeds of the Spirit: Wisdom of the Twentieth Century* eds. Richard H. Bell and Barbara L. Battin (Louisville: Westminster/ John Knox Press, 1995), 73.

8. See my discussion of "natural spirituality" in the introduction to *Seeds of the Spirit*, 14–22.

9. Vaclav Havel, *Living in Truth*, 31. Portions of the following account of Havel appeared in my *Simone Weil: The Way of Justice as Compassion*, 106–112.

10. British philosopher Peter Winch once remarked to me that he thought Havel's essay "The Power of the Powerless" was the most important piece of political philosophy of the twentieth century. Unusual and high praise for an artist denied his craft by his own people and exiled to work in a brewery in order to silence his power of the "word." In his exile, however, he managed to challenge his totalitarian state leaders and with others he quietly drew his people into an extraordinary revolution. He found a different way of thinking about justice in the surroundings of oppression and daily indignities and injustices; he managed to think and write his way through his predicament to emerge as a democratic civic leader of his country. We will see how he attributed the possibility of his success to his unfaltering belief in a spiritual horizon of humanity that transcended the boundaries dictated to him by his exiled condition.

11. Havel, *Living in Truth*, 15.

12. Havel, *Letters to Olga* (New York: Henry Holt and Company—An Owl Book, 1989), 123.

13. Havel, *Letters to Olga*, 147.

14. Havel, *Letters to Olga*, 231.

15. Havel, *Letters to Olga*, 243.

16. Havel, *Letters to Olga*, 301.

17. Havel, *Letters to Olga*, 370f. My emphasis.

18. Jean Bethke Elshtain, "A Man for This Season: Vaclav Havel on Freedom and Responsibility," unpublished manuscript. The same sentiment is noted about Havel in an earlier published essay by Elshtain where she says that his notion of an absolute or "higher horizon" opens up rather than forecloses genuine political responsibility. Havel's kind of morality in politics moves toward civic responsibility not away from it. Jean Bethke Elshtain, "Politics Without Cliché," *Social Thought* 60, no. 3 (Fall 1993): 436.

19. Havel, *Living in Truth*, 153. This passage has a similar prophetic ring to Stringfellow's words.

20. As found in *Pathways to Peace: Inter-religious Readings and Reflections*, ed. Jean Lesher (Cambridge, MA, Cowley Publications, 2005), 39f.

21. I would also say the same of Nelson Mandela in leading his oppressed majority of South Africans—also from exile. Though the South African revolution was not a "velvet one," and millions of its citizens suffered indignities and injustices greater

perhaps than did Havel's compatriots, South Africans found a way to a kind of justice that also sought to break the cycle of revenge and managed to give to all in their land the prospect for a new spirituality in their common search for justice.

22. Simone Weil, "The Legitimacy of the Provisional Government," trans. Peter Winch. *Philosophical Investigations* 10 no. 2 (April 1987): 87.

23. There are hints here of Stringfellow's theological idea of justice as a human practice stimulated by "Grace" in the context of the "Fall."

24. Simone Weil, *Selected Essays*, 53.

25. There were only hints of these more spiritually laden thoughts in her writings at the time of her political essays in *Oppression and Liberty* (1934) and in her early agonizing reflections on French colonialism. It was after three mystical religious experiences in 1938 that her writings took a more explicitly spiritual turn without losing sight of the importance of justice focusing attention on one's neighbor and the afflicted.

26. Simone Weil, *Waiting for God*, 139.

27. Simone Weil, *Waiting for God*, 140.

28. Simone Weil, *Waiting for God*, 143. My emphasis.

29. Simone Weil, *Waiting for God*, 151. My emphasis.

30. Simone Weil, *Notebooks*, 308.

31. Simone Weil, *First and Last Notebooks*, trans. Richard Rees (London: Oxford University Press, 1970), 103.

32. "A Carthusian," in Bell and Battin, *Seeds of the Spirit*, 60.

Epilogue

In separate instructions, Augustine told rulers to carry out their duty with such grace that their followers would obey them with pleasure. He argued that leaders ought to remember that they too were human and that they had weaknesses. They needed to control their desires, practice justice and mercy, and execute the law with love and kindness.

[Augustine, from *On Order* and *The City of God*][1]

The point to rethinking justice is to see if we as a human community are measuring up to the very task of being human. Are we engaged in helping rather than harming our fellow human beings? Have we arranged our civil life in order to enhance the respect and the dignity of persons near to us as well as to the distant stranger? How are we to "go up to someone," to "face" or "read" them without suspicion or malice? In ordering our communal affairs, our affairs of state, and our human affairs that cross boundaries, do we show a due sense of trust and respect for the other? Have we "measured" our relationship with others enough to know our obligations and when and how to reconcile differences with them? Do we have enough compassion and capacity for forgiveness to right wrongs and to initiate healing of broken relationships? To reflect on these questions is part of the process of rethinking justice. Each chapter in this book has tried to stick "close to the ground" of our common humanity—to look at those personal and public activities that bind us to one another as a human community.

We have "taken up residence" before the concept of justice. We have been responsive to its many demands. In our responsiveness we have encountered many voices that have added texture to the meaning of justice, rescuing it from its "thin," more "rule-governed" and more narrowly focused de-ontological and utilitarian accounts. We have looked at the grammar of justice through the lenses of its more "moral, spiritual, and aesthetic" aspects; through historical and political episodes, human testimony, and works of the literary and moral imagination.

In our radical rethinking of justice we have emphasized numerous concepts and connections that have fallen silent or have idled in the midst of our modern philosophical and political debates. Even worse, we have failed in our obligations to respect the dignity and sanctity of the lives of others. This has been particularly true of the unwarranted aggression of my own country, the United States. The concepts and connections that we have explored in rethinking justice and restoring our humanity were human dignity, mercy, and forgiveness, compassion, and restorative qualities within the democratic practices of a civil society. Following is a recapitulation of some of these concepts and ideas needed in our rethinking of justice as they were "emphasized" in the chapters of this book.

- *Justice appears in "that halt, that interval of hesitation, wherein lies all our consideration for our brothers in humanity."* [Simone Weil]
- *Our approach to "rethinking justice" is to surface what John Dunn called the human "moral, spiritual and aesthetic aspirations" in order to texture the debate more highly; to force our rethinking around concepts like trust, obligation, suffering and injustice, mercy, poverty, human dignity and equality, compassion and reconciliation.*
- *"In ordinary life kindness counts for more than belief in human rights."* [Jonathan Glover]
- *Justice is not simply found in the rule of law but in human social and moral practices that create a civil society.*
- *Embedded in the TRC process and their report is the making of a new "moral and spiritual" discourse and the call for a kind of justice called restorative justice that is intended to be the link between "truth" and "reconciliation," and that encourages both moral and social responsibility and such virtues as compassion, mercy and forgiveness, all for the purpose of helping to forge a new and more just South Africa.*
- *Justice comes in through a radical rethinking of the grammar of justice itself and through the process of human restoration that is understood to be as important as, and should become a part of, the rule of law in a time of difficult transition.*

When this kind of reciprocity in understanding becomes possible, then justice across boundaries is made possible. The face of the other is newly visible as my face, and my will to sympathetically understand, to trust, to forgive and to reconcile, all become enhanced. The degree to which my

moral and literary imagination can be heightened increases the prospect that there can be justice across boundaries.
- *Justice, and especially justice across boundaries (gender, race, nations, cultures, religious traditions) is a reflection of the kind of reciprocal acknowledgment of the humanness of the other whenever and wherever we "go up to them."* [Wittgenstein and Levinas]
- *"It is hard to understand how a compassionate world order can include so many people afflicted by acute misery, persistent hunger and deprived and desperate lives, and why millions of innocent children have to die each year from lack of food or medical attention or social care."* [Amartya Sen]
- *"What we need is for the spirit of justice to dwell within us. The spirit of justice is nothing other than the supreme and perfect flower of the madness of love."* [Simone Weil]
- *The work of justice and compassion go hand in hand. As do the work of justice and trust, justice and mercy, justice and development, and justice and reconciliation. These pairings cannot be torn asunder and retain the integrity of a meaningful concept of justice.*
- *"Habits of mind" essential for developing a just, deliberative democratic model: "belief in dialogue, respect for others, freedom from overweening ambition for power, and openness to mutual accommodations."* [Kwasi Wiredu]
- *Justice is the principal moral virtue for organizing human communities that enables the maximum of human freedom and dignity and that recognizes when harm arises or inequities endure, deliberative measures must be taken to restore a peaceful and equitable balance. Furthermore, as part of a just human community we are, in the words of Simone Weil, "obliged to safeguard the autonomy of others."*
- *It should be clear from the beginning of our journey—from Homer and Aeschylus, Socrates and Seneca to more recent conversations on rights and obligations, on retributive and restorative justice—that justice is neither simply a political concept nor only a modern secular idea. It is a deeply human concept. Justice is a testament to our humanity, not an individual demand for compensation or "getting one's due." . . . Justice reminds us that we have an obligation—a responsibility—to foster peace, to be merciful, and to promote reconciliation with our brothers and sisters in humanity. These are all essential to rethinking justice and to restoring our humanity.*

NOTE

1. As found in Elias K. Bongmba, *The Dialectics of Transformation in Africa*, 203.

Selected Bibliography

Appiah, Kwame Anthony. *In My Father's House: Africa in the Philosophy of Culture.* New York: Oxford University Press, 1992.

Appiah, Kwame Anthony. *The Ethics of Identity.* Princeton and Oxford: Princeton University Press, 2005.

Aung San Suu Kyi. "Freedom, Development, and Human Worth." *Journal of Democracy* 6, no. 2 (1995): 11–19.

Baier, Annette. "Trust and Antitrust." *Ethics,* 96 (January 1986) Chicago: University of Chicago Press.

Baldwin, James. "Fifth Avenue, Uptown." *Esquire,* (June 1960) Reprinted in Baldwin, *The Price of the Ticket.* New York: St. Martins, 1985.

Barber, Benjamin R. *Strong Democracy: Participatory Politics for a New Age.* Berkeley: University of California Press, 1984.

Bell, Richard H. *Simone Weil: The Way of Justice as Compassion.* Lanham, MD: Rowman & Littlefield, 1998.

———. *Understanding African Philosophy: A Cross-Cultural Approach.* New York: Routledge, 2002.

Bell, Richard H., ed. *Simone Weil's Philosophy of Culture.* Cambridge, UK: Cambridge University Press, 1993.

Bell, Richard H., guest editor. "African Philosophy and the Analytic Tradition." *Philosophical Papers*, 30, no. 3 (November 2001).

Bell, Richard H., and Barbara L. Battin, eds. *Seeds of the Spirit: Wisdom of the Twentieth Century.* Louisville, KY: Westminster/John Knox Press, 1995.

Bloom, Anthony. *Meditations: A Spiritual Journey through the Parables.* Denville, NJ: Dimension Books, 1972.

Bongmba, Elias K. *The Dialectics of Transformation in Africa.* New York: Palgrave Macmillan, 2006.

Boraine, Alec. *A Country Unmasked: Inside South Africa's Truth and Reconciliation Commission.* Oxford, UK: Oxford University Press, 2000.

Braithwaite, John. *Restorative Justice and Responsive Regulation.* Oxford, UK: Oxford University Press, 2002.

Braithwaite, John and Heather Strang. *Restorative Justice: Philosophy to Practice.* London and Burlington, VT: Ashgate Publishing Co., 2000.

———. *Restorative Justice and Civil Society.* Cambridge, UK: Cambridge University Press, 2001.

Brien, Andrew. "Mercy Within Legal Justice." *Social Theory and Practice* 24, no. 1 (Spring 1998).

Cavell, Stanley. *In Quest of the Ordinary: Lines of Skepticism and Romanticism.* Chicago: University of Chicago Press, 1988.

———. *This New Yet Unapproachable America: Lectures after Emerson after Wittgenstein.* Albuquerque, NM: Living Batch Press, 1989.

Coetzee, P. H., and A. J. P. Roux, eds. *Philosophy from Africa: A Text with Readings.* Cape Town, SA: Oxford University Press, 2002.

Crocker, David A. "Functioning and Capability: The Foundations of Sen's and Nussbaum's Development Ethic." *Political Theory* 20, no. 4 (November 1992).

———. "Functioning and Capability: The Foundations of Sen's and Nussbaum's Development Ethic, Part 2." *Women, Culture, and Development: A Study of Human Capabilities*, edited by Nussbaum and Jonathan Glover. Oxford: Clarendon Press, 1995.

———. "Hunger, Capability, and Development." In *World Hunger and Morality*, edited by William Aiken and Hugh La Follette. Upper Saddle River, NJ: Prentice Hall, 1996.

———. "Toward Development Ethics" *World Development* 19, no. 5 (1991).

Crocker, David A., and Toby Linden, eds. *Ethics of Consumption: The Good Life, Justice and Global Stewardship.* Lanham, MD, New York and London: Rowman & Littlefield, 1998.

de Gruchy, John W. *Reconciliation: Restoring Justice.* Minneapolis: Fortress Press, 2002.

Dunn, John. *Western Political Theory in the Face of the Future.* Cambridge, UK: Cambridge University Press, 1993.

Dworkin, Ronald M. *Freedom's Law: The Moral Reading of the American Constitution.* Cambridge, MA.: Harvard University Press, 1996.

Elshtain, Jean Bethke. "Politics Without Cliché." *Social Thought*, 60, no. 3 (Fall 1993).

Eze, Emmanuel C. *Achieving Our Humanity.* New York and London: Routledge, 2001.

Fanon, Frantz. *Toward the African Revolution.* New York: Monthly Review Press, 1988.

Gagiano, Annie. *Achebe, Head, Marechera.* Boulder, CO: Lynne Rienner Publishers, 2000.

Gaita, Raimond. *A Common Humanity: Thinking About Love and Truth and Justice.* London: Routledge, 2000.

Geertz, Clifford. *Interpretation of Cultures.* New York: Basic Books, 1973.

Glover, Jonathan. *Humanity: A Moral History of the Twentieth Century.* New Haven and London: Yale University Press, 2001.

Gobodo-Mandikizela, Pumla. *A Human Being Died That Night: A South African Story of Forgiveness.* Boston and New York: Houghton Mifflin Co., 2003.

Grayling, A. C. "Op Ed," *The Times Weekend Review,* March 13, 2004.

Greenawalt, Kent. "Amnesty's Justice." In *Truth V. Justice: The Morality of Truth Commissions,* edited by R. I. Rothberg and D. Thompson. Princeton and Oxford: Princeton University Press, 2002.

Gyekye, Kwame. *Tradition and Modernity: Philosophical Reflections on the African Experience.* New York and Oxford: Oxford University Press, 1997.

Hallie, Philip P. *Lest Innocent Blood Be Shed: The Story of the Village of Le Chambon and How Goodness Happened There.* San Francisco: Harper & Row, 1979.

——. *In the Eye of the Hurricane: Tales of Good and Evil, Help and Harm.* New York: HarperCollins Publishers, 1997.

Havel, Vaclav. *Letters to Olga.* New York: Henry Holt and Company, 1989.

——. *Living in Truth.* Edited by Jan Vladislaw. London: Faber and Faber, 1989.

Havelock, Eric A. *The Greek Concept of Justice: From Its Shadows in Homer to Its Substance in Plato.* Cambridge, MA and London: Harvard University Press, 1978.

Hayner, Priscilla. *Unspeakable Truths: Confronting State Terror and Atrocity.* New York and London: Routledge, 2001.

Head, Bessie. *Tales of Tenderness and Power.* Johannesburg, SA: A.D. Donker, 1989.

——. *A Woman Alone: Autobiographical Writings.* London: Heinemann, 1990.

Iliffe, John. *The African Poor.* Cambridge, UK: Cambridge University Press, 1989.

Irigaray, Luce. *Democracy Begins Between Two.* Translated by Kirsten Anderson. New York: Routledge, 2001.

——. *To Be Two.* Translated by Monique M. Rhodes and Marco F. Cocito-Monoc. New York: Routledge, 2001.

Kerr, Fergus. *Immortal Longings: Versions of Transcending Humanity.* London: SPCK, 1997.

Lesher, A. Jean. Pathways to Peace: Interreligious Readings and Reflections. Cambridge, MA: Cowley Publishers, 2005.

Levinas, Emmanuel. *The Levinas Reader.* Edited by Sean Hand. Oxford, UK: Basil Blackwell, 1989.

——. *Difficult Freedom: Essays on Judaism.* Translated by Sean Hand. Baltimore: Johns Hopkins University Press, 1990.

——. *Outside the Subject.* London: The Athlone Press, 1993.

Little, J. P. *Simone Weil: Waiting on Truth.* Berg Women's Series. Oxford, UK: St. Martin's Press, 1988.

——. *Simone Weil on Colonialism: An Ethic of the Other.* Edited and translated by J. P. Little. New York and Oxford: Rowman & Littlefield, 2003.

MacIntyre, Alasdair. *After Virtue: A Study in Moral Theory.* Notre Dame, IN: University of Notre Dame Press, 1981.

——. *Whose Justice? Which Rationality?* Notre Dame, IN: University of Notre Dame Press, 1988.

Mamdani, Mahmood. *Citizen and Subject: Contemporary Africa and the Legacy of Late Colonialism.* Princeton: Princeton University Press, 1996.

——. "A Diminished Truth." *Siyaya!* 3 (Spring 1998): 38–40.

Mandela, Nelson. *Long Walk to Freedom: The Autobography of Nelson Mandela.* Boston. Little, Brown, 1994.

May, Larry. *Sharing Responsibility.* Chicago: University of Chicago Press, 1992.

Minow, Martha. *Between Vengeance and Forgiveness: Facing History after Genocide and Mass Violence.* Boston: Beacon Press, 1998.

Mulhall, Stephen. *Stanley Cavell, Philosophy's Recounting of the Ordinary.* Oxford, UK: Oxford University Press, 1994.

N'Daye, Boubacar, Abdoulaye Saine, and Mathurin Hounjgnikpo. *Not Yet Democracy: West Africa's Slow Farewell to Authoritarianism.* Durham, NC: Carolina Academic Press, 2005.

Nozick, Robert. *Anarchy, State, and Utopia.* Oxford, UK: Basil Blackwell, 1974.

Nussbaum, Martha, and Amartya Sen, eds. *The Quality of Life.* New York: Oxford University Press, 1993.

Nussbaum, Martha. *Sex and Social Justice.* Oxford, UK: Oxford University Press, 1999.

O'Neill, Onora. *Bounds of Justice.* Cambridge, UK: Cambridge University Press, 2000.

——. *A Question of Trust.* Cambridge, UK: Cambridge University Press, 2002.

Pattison, George. *Kierkegaard: The Aesthetic and the Religious.* London: Macmillan, 1992.

Rawls, John. *A Theory of Justice.* Oxford, UK: Oxford University Press, 1971.

Rhees, Rush. *Discussions of Simone Weil.* Edited by D. Z. Phillips. Albany: State University of New York Press, 1999.

Rothberg, R. I., and D. Thompson, eds. *Truth V. Justice: The Morality of Truth Commissions.* Princeton and Oxford: Princeton University Press, 2002.

Sacks, Jonathan. *The Dignity of Difference: How to Avoid the Clash of Civilizations.* London, New York: Continuum, 2003.

Said, Edward. *Culture and Imperialism.* 2d ed. New York: Knopf: Distributed by Random House, 1994.

Sandel, Michael J. *Liberalism and the Limits of Justice.* 2d ed. Cambridge, UK: Cambridge University Press, 1998.

Sen, Amartya. *Inequality Reexamined.* Cambridge, MA.: Harvard University Press, 1995.

——. *Development as Freedom.* Oxford, UK: Oxford University Press, 1999.

Slye, Ronald C. "Amnesty, Truth, and Reconciliation." In *Truth V. Justice: The Morality of Truth Commissions,* Robert I. Rothberg and D. Thompson, 2002.

Solomon, Robert C., and Mark C. Murphy, eds. *What Is Justice: Classic and Contemporary Readings.* New York and Oxford: Oxford University Press, 2000.

Soyinka, Wole. "The Past Must Address Its Present," p. 19 in *Wole Soyinka: An Appraisal,* ed. Adewale Maja-Pearce. Oxford: Heinemann Educational Publishers, 1994.

——. Soyinka, Wole. "L. S. Senghor and Negritude," Chapter 2, in *The Burden of Memory, The Muse of Forgiveness*, New York and Oxford: Oxford University Press, 1999.

Stout, Jeffrey. *Democracy and Tradition*. Princeton: Princeton University Press, 2004.

Stringfellow, William. *The Politics of Spirituality*. Philadelphia: The Westminster Press, 1984.

Truth and Reconciliation Commission of South Africa, 5 vols. Cape Town, SA: Truth and Reconciliation Commission, 1998. Distributed by Cape Town: Juta & Company, and New York: Grove Dictionaries, 1999. The full report can be found online at www.truth.org.za. See especially vol. 1/5, sections 10–28 on "Promoting National Unity and Reconciliation." Also vol. 1/5 sections 66–69, 103, and 109.

Tutu, Desmond Mpilo. *No Future Without Forgiveness*. Armonk, NY: M. E. Sharpe, 2003.

Uchitelle, Louis. "How to Define Poverty? Let Us Count the Ways." *The New York Times*. May 26, 2001.

Verwoerd, Wilhelm. "Individual and/or Social Justice after Apartheid?" *The European Journal of Development Research* 11, no. 2 (December 1999).

——. "The TRC and Apartheid Beneficiaries in a New Dispensation." Published by the Centre for the Study of Violence and Reconciliation, January 19, 2003.

Verwoerd, Wilhelm, and Mahlubi "Chief" Mabizela, eds. *Truths Drawn in Jest: Commentary on the Truth and Reconciliation Commission through Cartoons*. Cape Town, SA: David Philips Publications, 2000.

Villa-Vicencio, Charles, and Wilhelm Verwoerd, eds. *Looking Back Reaching Forward*. Cape Town, SA: University of Cape Town Press, Zed Books Ltd., London, 2000.

Waldmeir, Patti, *Anatomy of a Miracle: The End of Apartheid and the Birth of the New South Africa*. New York: W. W. Norton & Co., 1997.

Waltzer, Michael. *Thick and Thin*. Notre Dame, IN: Notre Dame University Press, 1994.

Weil, Simone. *Waiting for God*. Translated by Emma Craufurd. New York: Harper Colophon Books, 1951.

——. *Notebooks*. Translated by Arthur Wills. London: Routledge & Kegan Paul, 1956. 2 vols.

——. *Selected Essays*: 1934–1943. Translated by Richard Rees. Oxford, UK: Oxford University Press, 1962.

——. *First and Last Notebooks*. Translated by Richard Rees. London: Oxford University Press, 1970.

——. *The Need for Roots*. Translated by Arthur Wills. New York: Harper Colophon Books, 1971.

——. *Gravity and Grace*. Translated by Emma Craufurd. London: Routledge & Kegan Paul, 1972.

——. *The Iliad or The Poem of Force*. Translated by Mary McCarthy. Wallingford, PA, Pendle Hill Pamphlet, no. 91 (1981).

140 *Selected Bibliography*

———. "Are We Struggling for Justice?" *Philosophical Investigations* 10, no. 1 (January 1987).
———. "The Legitimacy of the Provisional Government." Translated by Peter Winch. *Philosophical Investigations* 10, no. 2 (April 1987).
———. "Essay on the Notion of Reading." Translated by Rebecca Fine Rose and Timothy Tessin. *Philosophical Investigations* 13, no. 4 (October 1990).
Winch, Peter. *Simone Weil: "The Just Balance."* Cambridge, UK: Cambridge University Press, 1989.
Wiredu, Kwasi. *Cultural Universals and Particulars: An African Perspective.* Bloomington: Indiana University Press, 1996.
———. "The State, Civil Society and Democracy in Africa." *Quest* 12, no. 1 (1998).
Wittgenstein, Ludwig. *Philosophical Investigations.* London: The Macmillan Co., 1953.
Wolgast, Elizabeth. *The Grammar of Justice.* Ithaca, NY: Cornell University Press, 1987.
Zartman, I. William, ed. *Traditional Cures for Modern Conflicts: African Conflict "Medicine."* Boulder, CO: Lynne Rienner Publishers, 2000.

Index

About the Author

Richard H. Bell is Frank Halliday Ferris Professor of Philosophy Emeritus at The College of Wooster. Before coming to Wooster, Professor Bell received his B.D., M.A., and Ph.D. degrees at Yale University, where he also taught and was a dean of a Yale undergraduate college. He has authored numerous books and articles on or related to the thought of Simone Weil, Ludwig Wittgenstein and Søren Kierkegaard—as well as several books and articles on "spirituality." Most recently are his works: *Understanding African Philosophy: A Cross Cultural Approach to Classical and Contemporary Issues*, and *Simone Weil: The Way of Justice as Compassion*. Each of these works dealt with social and political aspects of justice that challenge traditional western ideas of justice and laid the groundwork for the present work.

The ideas in this book were conceived, drafted, and tested while teaching several seminars on the concept of justice at both The College of Wooster from 1998 to 2004 and during semesters of teaching honors and graduate seminars at Rhodes University in Grahamstown, South Africa, in August to November of 2004, and again in Grahamstown from July to December of 2006 while he was on a six-month Fulbright Senior Teaching and Research Grant.

He is grateful for conversations on early thoughts about this book with Wilhelm Verwoerd in Stellenbosch, South Africa and in Dublin, Ireland over the past six years, as well as with colleagues at Rhodes University over the past three years.